101 best campsites

for outdoor activities

alan rogers

Compiled by: Alan Rogers Guides Ltd

Designed by: Vine Design Ltd

© Alan Rogers Guides Ltd 2010

Published by: Alan Rogers Guides Ltd,
Spelmonden Old Oast, Goudhurst, Kent TN17 1HE
www.alanrogers.com
Tel: 01580 214000

British Library Cataloguing-in-Publication Data:
A catalogue record for this book is available from
the British Library.

ISBN 978-1-906215-35-4

Printed in Great Britain by
Stephens & George Print Group

contents

Welcome to the Alan Rogers
'101' guides

The Alan Rogers guides have been helping campers and caravanners make informed decisions about their holiday destinations since 1968. Today, whether online or in print, Alan Rogers still provides an independent, impartial view, with detailed reports on each campsite.

With so much unfiltered, unqualified information freely available, the Alan Rogers perspective is invaluable to make sure you make the right choice for your holiday.

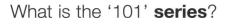

What is the '101' **series**?

At Alan Rogers, we know that readers have many and diverse interests, hobbies and particular requirements. And we know that our guides, featuring a total of some 3,000 campsites, can provide a bewildering choice from which it can be difficult to produce a shortlist of possible holiday destinations.

The Alan Rogers 101 guides are devised as a means of presenting a realistic, digestible number of great campsites, featured because of their suitability to a given theme.

This book remains first and foremost an authoritative guide to excellent campsites which offer great opportunities to enjoy a range of exciting outdoor activities.

101 **Best campsites for outdoor activities**

Campsites are all about being in the open air, enjoying wonderful natural surroundings. And, of course, time spent on a campsite lends itself to outdoor activities of all sorts, from 'conventional' sports like tennis, to activities often more associated with a holiday, such as kayaking or rafting, through to outward bound pursuits like orienteering and more specialist activities like sand yachting.

Recognising this, campsites have evolved hugely in recent years, investing in new sporting facilities, developing new services and attracting new activity-minded holiday makers.

This is partly due to leisure trends, partly to the influence of organisations like Center Parcs and the Duke of Edinburgh scheme and partly to commercial needs. Many campers are first and foremost activity enthusiasts, for whom staying on a campsite is simply a convenient means of enjoying their chosen activity. Others are 'die-hard' campers who also happen to enjoy a chosen activity.

Alan Rogers himself started off with the very specific aim of providing people with the necessary information to allow them to make an informed decision about their holiday destination. Today we still do that with a range of guides that now covers Europe's best campsites in 27 countries.

We work with campsites all day, every day. We visit campsites for inspection purposes (or even just for pleasure!). We know campsites 'inside out'.

We know which campsites would suit active families; which are great for get-away-from-it-all couples; we know which campsites are planning super new pool complexes; which campsites offer a fantastic menu in their on-site restaurant; which campsites allow you to launch a small boat from their slipway; which campsites have a decent playing area for kicking a ball around; which campsites have flat, grassy pitches and which have solid hard standings.

We also know which are good for fishing, golf, spas and outdoor activities; which are close to the beach; and which welcome dogs. These particular themes form our new '101' series.

All Alan Rogers guides (and our website) are respected for their independent, impartial and honest assessment. The reviews are prose-based, without overuse of indecipherable icons and symbols. Our simple aim is to help guide you to a campsite that matches best your requirements – often quite difficult in today's age of information overload.

What is the **best**?

The criteria we use when inspecting and selecting sites are numerous, but the most important by far is the question of good quality. People want different things from their choice of campsite, so campsite 'styles' vary dramatically: from small peaceful campsites in the heart of the countryside, to 'all singing, all dancing' sites in popular seaside resorts.

The size of the site, whether it's part of a chain or privately owned, makes no difference in terms of it being required to meet our exacting standards in respect of its quality and it being 'fit for purpose'. In other words, irrespective of the size of the site, or the number of facilities it offers, we consider and evaluate the welcome, the pitches, the sanitary facilities, the cleanliness, the general maintenance and even the location.

Expert opinions

We rely on our dedicated team of Site Assessors, all of whom are experienced campers, caravanners or motorcaravanners, to visit and recommend campsites. Each year they travel around Europe inspecting new campsites for Alan Rogers and re-inspecting the existing ones.

When planning
your **holiday...**

A holiday should always be a relaxing affair, and a campsite-based holiday particularly so. Our aim is for you to find the ideal campsite for your holiday, one that suits your requirements. All Alan Rogers guides provide a wealth of information, including some details supplied by campsite owners themselves, and the following points may help ensure that you plan a successful holiday.

Find out more

An Alan Rogers reference number (**e.g. FR12345**) is given for each campsite and can be useful for finding more information and pictures online at **www.alanrogers.com**
Simply enter this number in the 'Campsite Search' field on the Home page.

Campsite descriptions

We aim to convey an idea of its general appearance, 'feel' and features, with details of pitch numbers, electricity, hardstandings etc.

Facilities

We list specific information on the site's facilities and amenities and, where available, the dates when these facilities are open (if not for the whole season). Much of this information is as supplied to us and may be subject to change. Should any particular activity or aspect of the campsite be important to you, it is always worth discussing with the campsite before you travel.

Swimming pools

Opening dates, any charges and levels of supervision are provided where we have been notified. In some countries (notably France) there is a regulation whereby Bermuda-style shorts may not be worn in swimming pools (for health and hygiene reasons). It is worth ensuring that you do take 'proper' swimming trunks with you.

Charges

Those given are the latest provided to us, usually 2010 prices, and should be viewed as a guide only.

Toilet blocks

We assume that toilet blocks will be equipped with a reasonable number of British style WCs, washbasins and hot showers in cubicles. We also assume that there will be an identified chemical toilet disposal point, and that the campsite will provide water and waste water drainage points and bin areas. If not the case, we comment. We do mention certain features that some readers find important: washbasins in cubicles, facilities for babies, facilities for those with disabilities and motorcaravan service points.

Reservations

Necessary for high season (roughly mid-July to mid-August) in popular holiday areas (i.e. beach resorts). You can reserve many sites via our own Alan Rogers Travel Service or through other tour operators. Remember, many sites are closed all winter and you may struggle to get an answer.

Telephone numbers

All numbers assume that you are phoning from within the country in question. From the UK or Ireland, dial 00, then the country's prefix (e.g. France is 33), then the campsite number given, but dropping the first '0'.

Opening dates

Dates given are those provided to us and can alter before the start of the season. If you intend to visit shortly after a published opening date, or shortly before the closing date, it is wise to check that it will actually be open at the time required. Similarly, some sites operate a restricted service during the low season, only opening some of their facilities (e.g. swimming pools) during the main season; where we know about this, and have the relevant dates, we indicate it – again if you are at all doubtful it is wise to check.

Accommodation

Over recent years, more and more campsites have added high quality mobile homes, chalets, lodges, gites and more. Where applicable we indicate what is available and you'll find details online.

Special Offers

Some campsites have taken the opportunity to highlight a special offer. This is arranged by them and for clarification please contact the campsite direct.

The call of the
great **outdoors**

Campsites across Europe offer a huge range of outdoor activities, and this is the guide to help you find them. You may be a keen mountain biker or windsurfer; you may fancy trying white water rafting or sand yachting during your holiday; or you might simply be looking for a range of exciting activities for the kids this summer (away from the computer screen!).

Either way, there are campsites across Europe offering a chance to enjoy your chosen activity, or try something new. Get out there and give it a try!

Choosing campsites
for outdoor activities

The quality of sporting activities offered by campsites is often remarkable but it's clear that it is no longer enough for a well-run campsite to offer the bare minimum – proper investment, modern infrastructure, quality equipment and qualified professional supervision are all essential.

Convenience and choice

Some campsites offer a wide range of quality activities, aiming for wide appeal to all age groups and interests. This kind of campsite can be a great idea for families with different ages to cater for.

- Camping Ty Nadan in Brittany is exemplary, offering quad biking, aerial zip wires and tree top adventure trails, mountain biking, archery, paintballing and sea kayak excursions.

A specific speciality

Other campsites have become expert in a specific activity, perhaps by virtue of location or personal interest of the owner.

- Camping Wulfener Hals in northern Germany, is ideal for sailing and water sports.

- Camping l'Escale in the French Alps is a great base for a winter sports holiday.

- Camping Jungfrau in Switzerland, is ideal for climbing activities.

- Camping Seiser Alm in the Italian Dolomites and Glen Nevis Caravan and Camping Park in Scotland are great bases for mountain pursuits.

Regional specialities

Some people choose their campsite with a particular activity in mind.

- The lakes of the Landes in southwest France offer superb conditions for windsurfing.

- Many waterside campsites in Holland are popular with sailors for their facilities.

Something
for **everyone**

Swimming

Most family campsites these days boast a swimming pool, often an impressive aqua park with slides and pools. But for that 'at one with nature' feel, you can't beat splashing around in a river or lake. Try the tumbling waters of the Ardeche, with pebbly beaches and buzzards wheeling overhead above the craggy cliffs. Or enjoy the cool expanse of inviting waters of a shimmering English lake.

Adventure underground

Some campsites, especially in the Belgian Ardennes, are well placed for underground activities involving caves, potholes, ropes and flashlights.

Up in the trees…

A relatively recent innovation are aerial adventure parks, built up in the treetops of mature woodland. Increasing numbers of campsites have their own (Le Ty Nadan in Brittany).

Riding

Some campsites, like La Garangeoire in the Vendée, have their own stables and offer riding for all levels. Many others are close by riding facilities.

Canoeing

Canoeing is a great activity on many French campsites, especially in the Ardeche and Dordogne: it's easy to paddle downstream and fun for all the family. Some campsites offer proper tuition, then set you off with lunch and waterproof containers, arranging to meet you downstream and return you to the campsite by minibus (e.g Le Paradis in Dordogne).

Watersports

Many campsites are well-placed for sailing and windsurfing, some even have their own dinghy launching slipways. Others offer more esoteric activities like kite surfing, scuba diving and water skiing.

Skiing

Skiing is always popular and a little snow should never stop anyone from enjoying a camping holiday! A number of Alpine campsites in France, Austria, and Scandinavia, are open all year round and offer great skiing and snowboarding. Essentials like ski passes and equipment hire are often available while specially adapted mobile homes and accommodation are the norm.

Bikes

Road cycling is hugely popular and easily enjoyed while staying on a campsite. Off road trails for mountain bikes can be found, for example, at Natterersee in the Austrian Tirol.

'Experiences'

Of course, activities can be full-on adrenalin rushes or rather more sedate affairs. A majestic hot air balloon ride over the Loire chateaux, a dawn microlight flight or even an open air painting workshop make for a wonderful and memorable holiday experience.

Outdoor activities for
active **children**

Of course, children enjoy camping holidays at various levels. They enjoy the thrill of sleeping in a different environment; the freedom and fun; and all the small pleasures of being outdoors: pond dipping, watching wildlife, eating breakfast outside every morning. Activities do not always have to be organised.

Children's **Clubs**

Many campsites operate kids clubs in high season, usually free of charge and multi-national. Activities depend very much on age groups but usually include face painting, treasure hunts, rounders, swimming, circus skills and the like. Activities for older children might include paid-for canoe excursions, bike rides and discos and even rehearsals for a stage show in front of parents at the end of the week.

Qualified instruction...

It's not just the range of activities that is so impressive, it's the degree of professionalism of many campsites. Safety is taken seriously, with appropriate equipment and instruction.

Enjoy...!

Whether you're an 'old hand' or are contemplating your first trip, a regular reader of our Guides or a new 'convert', we wish you well in your travels and hope we have been able to help in some way. We are, of course, also out and about ourselves, visiting sites, talking to owners and readers, and generally checking on standards and new developments. We hope to bump into you!

Wishing you thoroughly enjoyable camping and caravanning in 2011 – favoured by good weather of course!

The Alan Rogers Team

Further **information**

And before you go...

Everyone has different expectations when it comes to holiday activities. And on holiday no-one wants nasty surprises. So be sure to check with the campsite that the activities offered are to your liking before you book.

Insurance

You will naturally have arranged travel insurance for your holiday (and if not, feel free to ask about our own Alan Rogers insurance on 01580 214006 or visit **www.alanrogers.com/travelinsurance**). If planning any dangerous activities please be sure you have appropriate cover.

SPAIN – Sant Pere Pescador

Camping La Gaviota

Ctra de la Platja s/n, E-17470 Sant Pere Pescador (Girona)
t: 972 520 569   e: info@lagaviota.com
alanrogers.com/ES80310   www.lagaviota.com

Accommodation: ☑Pitch ☑Mobile home/chalet ☐ Hotel/B&B ☐ Apartment

La Gaviota is a delightful, small, family run site at the end of a cul-de-sac with direct beach access. This ensures a peaceful situation with a choice of the pleasant L-shaped pool or direct beach access to the fine clean beach and slowly shelving access to the water. Everything here is clean and smart and the Gil family are very keen that you enjoy your time here. There are 165 touring pitches on flat ground with shade and electricity supply (6A). A lush green feel is given to the site by many palms and other semi-tropical trees and shrubs. The restaurant and bar are very pleasant indeed and have a distinct Spanish flavour. The cuisine is reasonably priced, perfectly prepared and served by friendly staff. All facilities are at the reception end of this rectangular site with extra washing up areas at the far end. The guests here were happy and enjoying themselves when we visited. English is spoken.

You might like to know
Sant Pere Pescador is an outstanding destination for windsurfers and kite surfers thanks to the Tramuntana and Garbi winds.

- ☑ Riding
- ☑ Cycling *(road)*
- ☑ Outdoor pool
- ☑ Crafts
- ☑ Sailing
- ☑ Windsurfing
- ☑ Kitesurfing
- ☑ Golf
- ☑ Kayaking
- ☑ Fishing

Facilities: One smart and very clean toilet block is near reception. All WCs are British style and the showers are excellent. Superb facilities for disabled visitors. Two great family rooms plus two baby rooms. Washing machine. Gas supplies. Supermarket (fresh bread). Pleasant bar and small, delightful restaurant. Swimming pool. Playground. Games room. Limited animation. Beach sports and windsurfing. Internet. Torches useful. ATM. Off site: Boat launching 2 km. Riding 4 km. Golf 15 km. Boat excursions. Cycling routes.

Open: 19 March - 24 October.

Directions: From the AP7/E15 take exit 3 onto the N11 north towards Figueras and then the C260 towards Roses. At Castello d'Empúries take the GIV 6216 and continue to Sant Pere Pescador. Site is well signed in the town. GPS: 42.18901, 3.10843

Charges guide

Per unit incl. 2 persons and electricity	€ 22,30 - € 50,70
extra person	€ 2,70 - € 3,90
child (under 10 yrs)	€ 1,40 - € 2,70
dog	€ 2,00 - € 4,00

No credit cards. Discounts for longer stays.

Camping Las Palmeras

Ctra de la Platja, E-17470 Sant Pere Pescador (Girona)
t: 972 520 506 e: info@campinglaspalmeras.com
alanrogers.com/ES80330 www.campinglaspalmeras.com

Accommodation: ☑Pitch ☑Mobile home/chalet ☐ Hotel/B&B ☐ Apartment

A very polished site, the pleasant experience begins as you enter the palm bedecked site and are greeted at the air conditioned reception building. The 230 pitches are flat, very clean and well maintained, with some shade and 10A electricity. A few pitches are complete with water and drainage. Thirty smart mobile homes are placed unobtrusively around the site. A very pleasant pool complex has a lifeguard and the brightly coloured play areas are clean and safe. The very pleasant beach is a 200 m. walk through a gate at the rear of the site. A full activities programme allows parents a break during the day and there is organised fun in the evenings in high season. The owner, Juan Carlos Alcantara, and his wife have many years experience in the campsite business which is clearly demonstrated. You will enjoy a stay here as there is a very happy atmosphere.

You might like to know

Las Palmeras is adjacent to the Punta de la Mora natural park, a great area for walking and cycling.

☑ Riding
☑ Tennis
☑ Cycling *(road)*
☑ Outdoor pool
☑ Crafts
☑ Sailing
☑ Windsurfing
☑ Kitesurfing
☑ Diving
☑ Waterskiing

☑ Golf
☑ Paintball
☑ Hiking
☑ Fitness/gym
☑ Go-karting

Facilities: Two excellent, very clean toilet blocks include first class facilities for disabled campers. Baby rooms. Facilities may become a little busy at peak periods. Washing machines. Motorcaravan services. Supermarket. Restaurant/bar (children's menu). Swimming pools (heated). Play areas. Tennis. Gym. Barbecue. Bicycle hire. Miniclub. Entertainment. Satellite TV. Internet access. ATM. Torches useful. Off site: Beach and fishing 200 m. Sailing and boat launching 2 km. Riding 4 km. Golf 7 km.

Open: 27 March - 23 October.

Directions: Sant Pere Pescador is south of Perpignan on coast between Roses and L'Escala. From the AP7/E15 take exit 4 onto the N11 north towards Figueres and then C31 towards Torroella de Fluvia. Take the Vilamacolum road east and continue to Sant Pere Pescador. Site well signed in town. GPS: 42.18805, 3.1027

Charges guide

Per unit incl. 2 persons and electricity	€ 21,70 - € 47,90
extra person	€ 2,50 - € 4,00
child (2-10 yrs)	€ 2,30
animal	€ 2,50 - € 4,00

SPAIN – Sant Pere Pescador

Camping Las Dunas

Ctra San Marti - Sant Pere, E-17470 Sant Pere Pescador (Girona)
t: **972 521 717**   e: **info@campinglasdunas.com**
alanrogers.com/ES80400   www.campinglasdunas.com

Accommodation: ☑Pitch ☑Mobile home/chalet ☐ Hotel/B&B ☐ Apartment

Las Dunas is an extremely large, impressive and well organised resort style site with many on–site activities and an ongoing programme of improvements. It has direct access to a superb sandy beach that stretches along the site for nearly a kilometre with a windsurfing school and beach bar. There is also a much used, huge swimming pool, plus a large double pool for children. Las Dunas is very large, with 1,700 individual hedged pitches (1,479 for tourers) of around 100 m² laid out on flat ground in long, regular parallel rows. All have electricity and 180 also have water and drainage. Shade is available in some parts of the site. Much effort has gone into planting palms and new trees here and the results are very attractive. The large restaurant and bar have spacious terraces overlooking the pools and you can enjoy a very pleasant, more secluded, cavern styled pub. A magnificent disco is close by in a soundproof building. With free quality entertainment of all types in season and positive security arrangements, this is a great site for families with teenagers. Member of Leading Campings Group.

You might like to know
On offer are also all types of adventure sports including canoeing, hot air balloon excursions, monoplane flights and gliding.

- ☑ Riding
- ☑ Tennis
- ☑ Cycling *(road)*
- ☑ Mountain biking
- ☑ Sports field
- ☑ Outdoor pool
- ☑ Crafts
- ☑ Archery
- ☑ Sailing
- ☑ Windsurfing

- ☑ Kitesurfing
- ☑ Diving
- ☑ Waterskiing
- ☑ Hiking
- ☑ Kayaking

Facilities: Five excellent large toilet blocks with electronic sliding glass doors (resident cleaners 07.00-21.00). Excellent facilities for youngsters, babies and disabled people. Laundry facilities. Motorcaravan services. Extensive supermarket, boutique and other shops. Large bar with terrace. Large restaurant. Takeaway. Ice cream parlour. Beach bar in main season. Disco club. Swimming pools. Playgrounds. Tennis. Archery. Minigolf. Sailing/windsurfing school and other watersports. Programme of sports, games, excursions and entertainment, partly in English (15/6-31/8). ATM. Safety deposit. Internet café. WiFi. Off site: Riding and boat launching 5 km. Water park 10 km. Golf 30 km. L'Escala 5 km.

Open: 19 May - 2 September.

Directions: L'Escala is northeast of Girona on the coast between Palamós and Roses. From A7/E15 autostrada take exit 5 towards L'Escala on GI 623. Turn north 2 km. before reaching L'Escala towards Sant Marti d'Ampúrias. Site is well signed. GPS: 42.16098, 3.13478

Charges guide

Per person	€ 3,50 - € 5,00
child (2-10 yrs)	€ 3,00 - € 3,25
pitch	€ 14,00 - € 52,00
dog	€ 3,20 - € 4,50

SPAIN – Sant Pere Pescador

Camping Aquarius

Playa s/n, E-17470 Sant Pere Pescador (Girona)
t: **972 520 003** e: **camping@aquarius.es**
alanrogers.com/ES80500 www.aquarius.es

Accommodation: ☑Pitch ☑Mobile home/chalet ☐ Hotel/B&B ☐ Apartment

A smart and efficient family site, Aquarius has direct access to a quiet sandy beach that slopes gently and provides good bathing (the sea is shallow for quite a long way out). Watersports are popular, particularly windsurfing (a school is provided). One third of the site has good shade with a park-like atmosphere. There are 435 pitches with electricity (6/16A). Markus Rupp and his wife are keen to make every visitor's experience a happy one. The site is ideal for those who really like sun and sea, with a quiet situation. The family is justifiably proud of their most attractive and absolutely pristine site which they continually upgrade and improve. The fountain at the entrance, the fishponds and the water features in the restaurant are soothing and pleasing. A small stage close to the restaurant is used for live entertainment in season. The spotless beach bar complex with shaded terraces, satellite TV and evening entertainment, has marvellous views over the Bay of Roses. The 'Surf Center' with rentals, school and shop is ideal for enthusiasts and beginners alike.

Special offers
Surf Centre on site specialising in wind- and kite-surfing offers courses with certified instructors for all levels.

You might like to know
Indoor and outdoor activity programme for all ages, all season. Children's Play Centre. Gym. Catamarans, snorkelling, water-trekking, creative crafts, go-karting and paintball are also on offer. Cultural excursions organised.

- ☑ Riding
- ☑ Archery
- ☑ Sailing
- ☑ Windsurfing
- ☑ Kitesurfing
- ☑ Diving
- ☑ Golf
- ☑ Canyoning
- ☑ Hot air ballooning
- ☑ Microlighting

- ☑ Boat tours
- ☑ Parachute jumps
- ☑ Beach volleyball
- ☑ Off-road cycling

Facilities: Attractively tiled, fully equipped, large toilet blocks provide some cabins for each sex. Excellent facilities for disabled people, plus baths for children. Superb new block has underfloor heating and family cabins. Laundry. Gas supplies. Motorcaravan services. Full size refrigerators. Supermarket. Pleasant restaurant and bar with terrace. Takeaway. Purpose built play centre for children (with qualified attendant), playground and separate play area for toddlers. TV room. 'Surf Center'. Minigolf. Bicycle hire. ATM. Internet access. WiFi. Dogs are accepted in one section. (Note: no pool). Off site: Fishing and boat launching 3 km. Riding 6 km. Golf 15 km.

Open: 15 March - 31 October.

Directions: From the AP7/E15 take exit 4 onto N11 north towards Figueras and then the C31 towards Torroella de Fluvia. Take the Vilamacolum road east and continue to Sant Pere Pescador. Site well signed in town. GPS: 42.1769, 3.10797

Charges guide

Per person	€ 3,00 - € 4,00
child (under 12 yrs)	free - € 2,65
pitch incl. electricity	€ 8,80 - € 44,50

Discounts for pensioners on longer stays.
No credit cards.

SPAIN – Sant Pere Pescador

Camping La Ballena Alegre

E-17470 Sant Pere Pescador (Girona)
t: **902 510 520** e: **infb2@ballena-alegre.com**
alanrogers.com/ES80600 www.ballena-alegre.com

Accommodation: ☑Pitch ☑Mobile home/chalet ☐Hotel/B&B ☐Apartment

La Ballena Alegre is partly in a lightly wooded setting, partly open, and has almost 2 km. of frontage directly onto an excellent beach of soft golden sand (which is cleaned daily). They claim that none of the 1,531 touring pitches is more than 100 m. from the beach. The grass pitches are numbered and there is a choice of size (up to 100 m²). Electrical connections (5/10A) are available in all areas and there are 378 fully serviced pitches. A recent addition is a resort village area within the site with holiday homes and its own small pool and play area. This is a great site for families. There are restaurant and bar areas beside the pleasant terraced pool complex (four pools including a pool for children). For those who wish to drink and snack late there is a pub open until 03.00 hrs. The well managed soundproofed disco is popular with youngsters. A little train ferries people along the length of the site and a road train runs to local villages. Plenty of entertainment and activities are offered, including a well managed watersports centre, with sub-aqua, windsurfing and kite-surfing.

You might like to know
Best conditions to practise wind- and kite-surfing. Host since 1999 of the PWA Windsurf-World Cup. In 2010 host for the first time for the 29th European championships. Club Mistral provides lessons and hire of windsurf and kite-surfing equipment.

- ☑ Tennis
- ☑ Mountain biking
- ☑ Sports field
- ☑ Outdoor pool
- ☑ Crafts
- ☑ Sailing
- ☑ Windsurfing
- ☑ Kitesurfing
- ☑ Waterskiing
- ☑ Kayaking

- ☑ Fitness/gym
- ☑ Fishing

Facilities: Seven well maintained toilet blocks are of a very high standard. Facilities for children, babies and disabled campers. Launderette. Motorcaravan services. Gas supplies. Supermarket. 'Linen' restaurant. Self-service restaurant and bar. Takeaway. Pizzeria and beach bar in high season. Swimming pool complex. Jacuzzi. Tennis. Watersports centre. Fitness centre. Bicycle hire. Playgrounds. Sound proofed disco. Dancing twice weekly and organised activities, sports, entertainment, etc. ATM. In high season dogs only allowed in one zone (26/6-22/8). Internet access and WiFi. Torches useful in beach areas. Off site: Go-karting nearby with bus service. Fishing 300 m. Riding 2 km.

Open: 14 May - 20 September.

Directions: From A7 Figueres - Girona autopista take exit 5 to L'Escala GI 623 for 18.5 km. At roundabout take sign to Sant Marti d'Empúries and follow site signs. GPS: 42.15323, 3.11248

Charges guide

Per unit incl. 2 persons and electricity	€ 25,00 - € 70,00
extra person	€ 3,75 - € 4,54
child (3-9 yrs)	€ 2,70 - € 3,28
dog	€ 2,25 - € 4,74

No credit cards.

SPAIN – Calonge

Camping Internacional de Calonge

Ctra San Feliu/Guixols - Palamós, E-17251 Calonge (Girona)
t: **972 651 233**   e: **info@intercalonge.com**
alanrogers.com/ES81300   www.intercalonge.com

Accommodation: ☑Pitch ☑Mobile home/chalet ☐ Hotel/B&B ☐ Apartment

This spacious, well laid out site has access to a fine beach by a footbridge over the coast road, or you can take the little road train as the site is on very sloping ground. Calonge is a family site with two good sized pools on different levels, a paddling pool and large sunbathing areas. A great restaurant, bar and snack bar are by the pool. The site's 793 pitches are on terraces and all have electricity (5A), with 84 being fully serviced. The pitches are set on attractively landscaped terraces (access to some may be challenging). There is good shade from the tall pine trees and some views of the sea through the foliage. The views from the upper levels are taken by the tour operator and mobile home pitches. The pools are overlooked by the restaurant terraces which have great views over the mountains. A nature area within the site is used for walks or picnics. A separate area within the site is set aside for visitors with dogs (including a dog shower!) The beach is accessed over the main road by a bridge and 100 steps and is shared with another campsite.

Special offers
For this year's special offers contact the site.

You might like to know
One of the finest sites on the Costa Brava, celebrating its 50th anniversary this year.

☑ Riding
☑ Tennis
☑ Cycling (road)
☑ Mountain biking
☑ Sports field
☑ Outdoor pool
☑ Sailing
☑ Windsurfing
☑ Diving
☑ Golf

☑ Hiking
☑ Kayaking
☑ Sports area
☑ Fishing

Facilities: Generous sanitary provision in new or renovated blocks include some washbasins in cabins. No toilet seats. One block is heated in winter. Laundry facilities. Motorcaravan services. Gas supplies. Shop (27/3-31/10), Bar/restaurant, patio bar, pizza and takeaway (all 27/3-24/10, weekends for the rest of the year). Swimming pools (27/3-12/10). Playground. Electronic games. Rather noisy disco two nights a week (but not late). Bicycle hire. Tennis. Hairdresser. ATM. Internet access and WiFi. Road train from the bottom of the site to the top in high season. Off site: Bus at the gate. Fishing 300 m. Supermarket 500 m. Golf 3 km. Riding 10 km.

Open: All year.

Directions: Site is on the inland side of the coast road between Palamós and Platja d'Aro. Take the C31 south to the 661 at Calonge. At Calonge follow signs to the C253 towards Platja d'Aro and on to the site. GPS: 41.83333, 3.08417

Charges guide

Per unit incl. 2 persons and electricity	€ 19,65 - € 44,65
extra person	€ 3,65 - € 7,85
child (3-10 yrs)	€ 1,85 - € 4,40
dog	€ 3,20 - € 4,05

No credit cards.

Camping Roche

N340 km 19,5, Carril de Pilahito, E-11140 Conil de la Frontera (Cádiz)
t: 956 442 216 e: info@campingroche.com
alanrogers.com/ES88590 www.campingroche.com

Accommodation: ☑Pitch ☑Mobile home/chalet ☐Hotel/B&B ☐Apartment

Camping Roche is situated in a pine forest near white sandy beaches in the lovely region of Andalucia. It is a clean and tidy, welcoming site. Little English is spoken but try your Spanish, German or French as the staff are very helpful. A family site, it offers a variety of facilities including a sports area and swimming pools. The restaurant has good food and a pleasant outlook over the pool. Games are organised for children. A recently built extension provides further pitches, a new toilet block and a tennis court. There are now 335 pitches which include 104 bungalows to rent. There are pleasant paths in the area for mountain biking and this is an ideal base for visiting the cities of Seville and Cádiz.

You might like to know
The cities of Seville and Cadiz are both within easy reach for interesting day trips.

- ☑ Riding
- ☑ Pony trekking
- ☑ Tennis
- ☑ Cycling (road)
- ☑ Sports field
- ☑ Outdoor pool
- ☑ Sailing
- ☑ Surfing
- ☑ Windsurfing
- ☑ Kitesurfing

- ☑ Diving
- ☑ Golf
- ☑ Hiking
- ☑ Fitness/gym
- ☑ Fishing

Facilities: Three toilet blocks are traditional in style and provide simple, clean facilities. Washbasins have cold water only. Washing machine. Supermarket. Bar and restaurant. Swimming and paddling pools. Sports area. Tennis. Play area. Off site: Bus stops 3 times daily outside gates.

Open: All year.

Directions: From the N340 (Cádiz - Algeciras) turn off to site at km. 19.5 point. From Conil, take El Pradillo road. Keep following signs to the site. From CA3208 road turn at km. 1 and site is 1.5 km. down this road on the right.
GPS: 36.31089, -6.11268

Charges guide

Per unit incl. 2 persons and electricity	€ 33,00
extra person	€ 6,50
child	€ 5,50
dog	€ 3,75

Low season discounts.

Camping Picos de Europa

E-33556 Avin-Onis (Asturias)
t: 985 844 070 e: info@picos-europa.com
alanrogers.com/ES89650 www.picos-europa.com

Accommodation: ☑Pitch ☑Mobile home/chalet ☐Hotel/B&B ☑Apartment

This delightful site is, as its name suggests, an ideal spot from which to explore these dramatic limestone mountains on foot, by bicycle or on horseback. The site itself is continuously developing and the dynamic owner, José, or his nephew who helps out when he is away, are both very pleasant and nothing is too much trouble. The site is in a valley beside a pleasant, fast flowing river. The 160 marked pitches are of varying sizes and have been developed in three avenues, on level grass mostly backing on to hedging, with 6A electricity. An area for tents and apartments is over a bridge past the fairly small, but pleasant, round swimming pool. Local stone has been used for the L-shaped building at the main entrance which houses reception and a very good bar/restaurant. The site can organise caving activities, and has information about the Cares gorge along with the many energetic ways of exploring the area, including by canoe and quad-bike! The Bulnes funicular railway is well worth a visit.

You might like to know

White water canoeing at the Sella descent offers different starting points giving courses from 6 km. to 14 km. and provides one, two or three seat canoes.

- ☑ Riding
- ☑ Mountain biking
- ☑ Outdoor pool
- ☑ Rafting
- ☑ Canyoning
- ☑ Potholing
- ☑ Hiking
- ☑ Aerial walkways
- ☑ Canoeing
- ☑ Kayaking

Facilities: Toilet facilities include a new fully equipped block, along with new facilities for disabled visitors and babies. Pleasant room with tables and chairs for poor weather. Washing machine and dryer. Shop (July-Sept). Swimming pool (Feb-Sept). Bar and cafeteria style restaurant (all year) serves a good value 'menu del dia' and snacks. WiFi in restaurant area. Play area. Fishing. Torches necessary in the new tent area. Off site: Riding 12 km. Bicycle hire 15 km. Golf 25 km. Coast at Llanes 25 km.

Open: All year.

Directions: Avin is 15 km. east of Cangas de On's on AS114 road to Panes and is probably best approached from this direction especially if towing. From A8 (Santander - Oviedo) use km. 326 exit and N634 northwest to Arriondas. Turn southeast on N625 to Cangas and join AS114 (Covodonga/Panes) by-passing Cangas. Site is just beyond Avin after 16 km. marker. GPS: 43.3363, -4.94498

Charges guide

Per person	€ 5,02
child (under 14 yrs)	€ 4,01
pitch incl. car	€ 8,57 - € 9,64
electricity	€ 3,75

PORTUGAL – Póvoa de Varzim

Orbitur Camping Rio Alto

EN13 km 13 Rio Alto-Est, Estela, P-4570-275 Póvoa de Varzim (Porto)
t: **252 615 699** e: **info@orbitur.pt**
alanrogers.com/PO8030 www.orbitur.pt

Accommodation: ☑Pitch ☑Mobile home/chalet ☐Hotel/B&B ☐Apartment

This site makes an excellent base for visiting Porto which is some 35 km. south of
Estela. It has around 700 pitches on sandy terrain and is next to what is virtually
a private beach. There are some hardstandings for caravans and motorcaravans and
electrical connections to most pitches (long leads may be required). The area for tents
is furthest from the beach and windswept, stunted pines give some shade. There
are arrangements for car parking away from camping areas in peak season. There is
a quality restaurant, snack bar and a large swimming pool across the road from
reception. An 18 hole golf course is adjacent and huge nets along one side of the site
protect campers from any stray balls. The beach is accessed via a novel double tunnel
in two lengths of 40 metres under the dunes (open 09.00-19.00). The beach shelves
steeply at some tidal stages (lifeguard 15/6-15/9).

You might like to know
The first European campsite to be certified
for service quality standards by SGS ICS. Rio
Alto has direct access to a fine beach through
a tunnel beneath the dunes and a golf course
in the middle of Portugal's Green Coast.

☑ Riding
☑ Tennis
☑ Cycling (road)
☑ Sports field
☑ Outdoor pool
☑ Sailing
☑ Windsurfing
☑ Golf
☑ Kayaking
☑ Fishing

Facilities: Four refurbished and well equipped
toilet blocks have hot water. Laundry facilities.
Facilities for disabled campers. Gas supplies.
Shop (1/6-31/10). Restaurant, bar, snack bar
(1/5-31/10). Swimming pool (1/6-30/9). Tennis.
Playground. Games room. Surfing. TV. Medical
post. Car wash. Evening entertainment twice
weekly in season. Off site: Fishing. Golf. Bicycle
hire. Riding (all within 5 km).

Open: All year.

Directions: From A28 in direction of Porto, leave
at exit 18 s.p. Fao/Apuila. At roundabout take
N13 in direction of Pavoa de Varzim/Porto for
2.5 km. At Hotel Contriz, turn right onto narrow
cobbled road. Site well signed in 2 km.
GPS: 41.44504, -8.75767

Charges guide

Per person	€ 2,90 - € 5,40
child (5-10 yrs)	€ 1,50 - € 3,00
caravan and car	€ 6,80 - € 12,00
electricity (5/15A)	€ 2,50 - € 3,10

Off season discounts (up to 70%).

PORTUGAL – Odemira

Zmar-Eco Camping Resort

Herdade ç de Mateus E.N. 393/1, San Salvador, P-7630 Odemira (Beja)
t: **707 200 626** e: **info@zmar.eu**
alanrogers.com/PO8175 www.zmar.eu

Accommodation: ☑Pitch ☑Mobile home/chalet ☐Hotel/B&B ☐Apartment

Zmar is an exciting new project which should be fully open this year. The site is located near Zambujeira do Mar, on the Alentejo coast. This is a highly ambitious initiative developed along very strict environmental lines. Public indoor spaces have no air-conditioning, but there is adequate cooling through underfloor ventilation and electric fans where possible. Pitches are of 100 m² and benefit from artificial shade. Caravans and wood-clad mobile homes are also available for rent. The swimming pool complex features a large outdoor pool and an indoor pool area with a wave machine and a 'wellness' centre. The very large and innovative children's play park has climbing nets, labyrinths and caves. There is also a children's farm and a large play house. For adults, many sporting amenities will be available around the resort's 81 hectare park. These will include a sports field, bicycle hire, tennis courts under a huge tent and a military-style climbing and abseiling adventure installation.

You might like to know
On the campsite you will find a Centre for Environmental Interpretation that shows and explains the fauna, flora and climate of the region and its main historical remains.

- ☑ Tennis
- ☑ Mountain biking
- ☑ Sports field
- ☑ Outdoor pool
- ☑ Archery
- ☑ Hiking
- ☑ Canoeing
- ☑ Fitness/gym
- ☑ Fishing
- ☑ Treetop Adventures

Facilities: Eight toilet blocks provide comprehensive facilities for all including for children and disabled visitors. Bar. Restaurant. Crêperie. Takeaway food. Large supermarket. Swimming pool. Covered pool. Wellness centre. Sports field. Games room. Play area, farm and play house. Tennis. Bicycle hire. Activity and entertainment programme. Mobile homes and caravans for rent. Caravan repair and servicing. The site's own debit card system is used for payment at all facilities. Off site: Vicentina coast and the Alentejo natural park. Sines (birthplace of Vasco de Gama). Cycle and walking tracks. Sea fishing.

Open: All year.

Directions: From the N120 from Odemira to Lagos, at roundabout in the centre of Portas de Transval turn towards Milfontes. Take turn to Cabo Sard‹o and then Zambujeira do Mar. Site is on the left. GPS: 37.60422, -8.73142

Charges guide

Per unit incl. 1-4 persons and electricity	€ 20,00 - € 50,00
extra person	€ 5,00 - € 10,00
child (4-12 yrs)	€ 5,00

ITALY – Grado

Camping Tenuta Primero

Via Monfalcone 14, I-34073 Grado (Friuli - Venézia Giúlia)
t: **043 189 6900** e: **info@tenuta-primero.com**
alanrogers.com/IT60065 www.tenuta-primero.com

Accommodation: ☑Pitch ☑Mobile home/chalet ☐ Hotel/B&B ☐ Apartment

Tenuta Primero was established in 1962 and has been a popular family site ever since. The third generation of the Marzola family continue to run the site and have made many improvements over the years. This is a large site with its own private beach and 800 pitches of varying sizes, including some new, large 'executive' pitches, with beach front locations, 10A electricity and a private water supply. Nine toilet blocks are dispersed around the site, some equipped with facilities for disabled visitors. There are no fewer than three restaurants here (including a pizzeria and a fish restaurant) and two bars, as well as a separate disco. Alongside the campsite is a large private marina with moorings for over 200 boats and a maintenance area. Tenuta Primero also comprises an 18-hole championship golf course and a nine-hole executive course. Special rates are available for campers. Grado is a fascinating resort 5 km. distant. The old town predates Venice and has a similar appeal.

You might like to know

There is an adjacent 27-hole golf course and no fewer than three restaurants here.

☑ Riding
☑ Tennis
☑ Short tennis
☑ Cycling *(road)*
☑ Sports field
☑ Outdoor pool
☑ Archery
☑ Sailing
☑ Windsurfing
☑ Kitesurfing

☑ Golf
☑ Aerial walkways
☑ Canoeing
☑ Kayaking
☑ Pedaloes

Facilities: Supermarket. Bars and restaurants. Pizzeria. Swimming and paddling pools. Disco. Beauty salon. Aerobics and aquagym. Windsurfing and sailing lessons. Play area. Sports pitches. Bicycle hire. Entertainment and activity programme. Children's activities. Direct access to beach. Mobile homes and chalets for rent. Dogs are not accepted. Off site: Campsite harbour. Two golf courses. Cycle track to Grado. Shops, restaurants and bars in Grado. Riding 2 km.

Open: 1 April - 4 October.

Directions: Take the Palmanova exit from the A4 autostrada and drive to Grado on the SS352 passing through Aquileia and Cervignano. Continue towards Monfalcone on the SP19 and the site can be found on the right after 5 km. GPS: 45.7051, 13.4640

Charges guide

Per person	€ 5,00 - € 11,00
child (3-11 yrs)	free - € 7,00
child (12-15 yrs)	€ 4,00 - € 9,00
pitch incl. electricity	€ 10,00 - € 25,00

ITALY – Rasen

Camping Corones

I-39030 Rasen (Trentino - Alto Adige)
t: 047 449 6490 e: info@corones.com
alanrogers.com/IT61990 www.corones.com

Accommodation: ☑Pitch ☑Mobile home/chalet ☐ Hotel/B&B ☑Apartment

Situated in a pine forest clearing at the foot of the attractive Antholz valley in the heart of German-speaking Südtirol, Corones is ideally situated both for winter sports enthusiasts and for walkers, cyclists, mountain bikers and those who prefer to explore the valleys and mountain roads of the Dolomites by car. There are 135 level pitches, all with electricity (16A) and many also with water and drainage and satellite TV. The Residence offers luxury apartments and there are authentic Canadian log cabins for hire. The bar/restaurant and small shop are open all season. From the site you can see slopes which in winter become highly rated skiing pistes. A short drive up the broad Antholz (Anterselva) valley takes you to an internationally important biathlon centre. A British couple who were on site when we visited had just driven up the valley and over the pass into Austria and then back via another pass. Back on site, a small pool and paddling pool could be very welcome. There is a regular programme of free excursions and occasional evening events are organised.

Special offers
Free Skibus. Family deals. White weeks.
Children's activity programme (in summer).

You might like to know
Plenty of activities on site with something for everyone: tranquil spots for those wanting to relax in the fresh air and many opportunities for those seeking activities and adventure.

- ☑ Riding
- ☑ Tennis
- ☑ Golf
- ☑ Rock climbing
- ☑ Hiking
- ☑ Skiing *(downhill)*
- ☑ Skiing *(cross-country)*
- ☑ Snowboarding
- ☑ Aerial walkways
- ☑ Climbing wall

- ☑ Guided walks
- ☑ Ski-safari
- ☑ Snowshoeing
- ☑ Fishing
- ☑ Cycling
  (road/off-road)

Facilities: The central toilet block is traditional but well maintained and clean. Additional facilities below the Residence are of the highest quality including individual shower rooms with washbasins, washbasins with all WCs, a delightful children's unit and an excellent facility for disabled visitors. Luxurious wellness centre with saunas, solarium, jacuzzis, massage, therapy pools and heat benches. Heated outdoor swimming and paddling pools (4/5-20/10). Play area. Internet facilities. Off site: Tennis 800 m. Bicycle hire 1 km. Riding and fishing 3 km. Golf (9 holes) 10 km. Canoeing/kayaking 15 km.

Open: 6 December - 30 March,
4 May - 31 October.

Directions: Rasen/Rasun is 85 km. northeast of Bolzano. From Bressanone/Brixen exit on the A22 Brenner - Modena motorway, go east on the SS49 for 50 km. Then turn north (signed Razen/Antholz). Turn immediately west at roundabout in Niederrasen/Rasun di Sotto to site on left in 100 m. GPS: 46.7758, 12.0367

Charges guide

Per unit incl. 2 persons and electricity	€ 18,50 - € 26,70
extra person	€ 4,50 - € 7,30
child (3-15 yrs)	€ 3,00 - € 5,90

ITALY – Völs am Schlern

Camping Seiser Alm

Saint Konstantin 16, I-39050 Völs am Schlern (Trentino - Alto Adige)
t: **047 170 6459** e: **info@camping-seiseralm.com**
alanrogers.com/IT62040 www.camping-seiseralm.com

Accommodation: ☑Pitch ☑Mobile home/chalet ☐ Hotel/B&B ☐ Apartment

What an amazing experience awaits you at Seiser Alm! Elisabeth and Erhard Mahlknecht have created a superb site in the magnificent Südtirol region of the Dolomite mountains. Towering peaks provide a magnificent backdrop when you dine in the charming, traditional style restaurant on the upper terrace. Here you will also find the bar, shop and reception. The 150 touring pitches are of a very high standard with 16A electricity supply, 120 with gas, water, drainage and satellite connections. Guests were delighted with the site when we visited, many coming to walk or cycle, some just to enjoy the surroundings. There are countless things to see and do here. Enjoy the grand 18-hole golf course alongside the site or join the plethora of excursions and organised activities. Local buses and cable cars provide an excellent service for summer visitors and skiers alike. In keeping with the natural setting, the majority of the luxury facilities are set into the hillside. If you wish for quiet, quality camping in a crystal clean environment, then visit this immaculate site.

You might like to know

The Seiser Alm campsite is located in Alpe di Siusi and overlooks a wonderful landscape with a fine view of the towering Sciliar Massif the symbol of Alto Adige.

☑ Riding
☑ Pony trekking
☑ Golf
☑ Rock climbing
☑ Hiking
☑ Aerial walkways
☑ Climbing wall
☑ Microlighting
☑ 10-pin bowling
☑ Model gliders

☑ Paragliding
☑ Hang-gliding
☑ Skiing
☑ Snowboarding

Facilities: One luxury underground block is in the centre of the site. 16 private units are available. Excellent facilities for disabled visitors. Fairy tale facilities for children. Washing machines and large drying room. Sauna. Supermarket. Quality restaurant and bar with terrace. Entertainment programme. Miniclub. Children's adventure park and play room. Special rooms for ski equipment. Torches useful. Off site: Riding alongside site. Golf 18-hole course (discounts) 1 km. Fishing 1 km. Bicycle hire 2 km. Lake swimming 2 km. ATM 3 km. Walks. Skiing in winter. Buses to cable cars and ski lifts.

Open: All year excl. 5 November - 20 December.

Directions: Site is east of Bolzano. From the A22-E45 take Bolzano Nord exit. Take road for Prato Isarco/Blumau, then road for Fie/Vols. Take care as the split in the road is sudden and if you miss the left fork as you enter a tunnel (Altopiano dello Sciliar/Schlerngebiet) you pay a heavy price in extra kilometres. Enjoy the climb and site is well signed. GPS: 46.53344, 11.53335

Charges guide

Per person	€ 6,00 - € 8,50
child (2-15 yrs)	€ 3,40 - € 6,80
pitch	€ 3,00 - € 11,00
electricity (per kWh)	€ 0,60

ITALY – Pozza di Fassa

Camping Vidor Resort

Strada de Ruf de Ruacia 19, I-38036 Pozza di Fassa (Trentino - Alto Adige)
t: **046 276 0022** e: **info@campingvidor.it**
alanrogers.com/IT62090 www.campingvidor.it

Accommodation: ☑Pitch ☑Mobile home/chalet ☐ Hotel/B&B ☐ Apartment

This family run site is in a natural setting two kilometres from the town of Pozza. Vidor received some major upgrading in 2008 with a brand new building housing reception, a camping shop, restaurant and pizzeria, and a café with terrace and lounge. There is an indoor heated swimming pool (with whirlpool etc) and beauty and 'wellness' centres offering a large variety of treatments and a fitness room. Indoor playrooms for children and teenagers, a miniclub, a TV room, cinema and conference room, internet corner and a cash machine complete this first class provision. These facilities augment the existing excellent sanitary facilities. The pitches are of average size (with 16A electricity, water and drain) plus some fully serviced pitches (with hardstanding and 16A electricity), are in an attractive setting. There are some slopes so chocks are advisable. A hundred metres from the site a large restaurant serves local cuisine. The local area is excellent for hiking in summer and skiing in winter.

Special offers
Special rates with local ski schools and ski rental agencies. Special discounts on lift passes.

You might like to know
Guided tours and climbing lessons are available. Ski passes can be bought at reception.

☑ Riding
☑ Cycling *(road)*
☑ Mountain biking
☑ Golf
☑ Rock climbing
☑ Hiking
☑ Skiing *(downhill)*
☑ Skiing *(cross-country)*
☑ Snowboarding
☑ Snowshoeing

☑ Climbing wall
☑ Fishing
☑ Fitness & aquagym
☑ Paragliding

Facilities: Two excellent hotel standard sanitary blocks provide hot water throughout and good showers with private bathrooms for hire. Facilities for disabled visitors. Washing machines, drying room and dryer. Bar/restaurant, takeaway and shop. Beauty and wellness centre, heated indoor pool and gym (all season). TV room and cinema. Indoor playrooms and miniclub. WiFi over whole site. Entertainment programme. Off site: Town 2 km. with usual facilities. Fishing 500 m. Ski lift 1 km. Golf 8 km. Hiking. Many excursions to places of interest.

Open: All year except November.

Directions: From A22 Trento - Bolzano road take S48 to Pozza di Fassa. Take the road south to Meida and Valle S Nicola. Cross the bridge and site is well signed in 2 km.
GPS: 46.41987, 11.70754

Charges guide

Per person	€ 6,50 - € 8,50
child (10-15 yrs)	€ 6,00 - € 8,00
child (2-10 yrs)	€ 5,00 - € 7,00
pitch	€ 7,50 - € 15,00
dog	€ 3,00 - € 4,00

ITALY – Lévico Terme
Camping Lévico

Localitá Pleina 5, I-38056 Lévico Terme (Trentino - Alto Adige)
t: 046 170 6491   e: mail@campinglevico.com
alanrogers.com/IT62290   www.campinglevico.com

Accommodation: ☑Pitch ☑Mobile home/chalet ☐ Hotel/B&B ☐ Apartment

Sister site to Camping Jolly, Camping Lévico is in a natural setting on the small, very pretty Italian lake also called Lévico which is surrounded by towering mountains. The sites are owned by two brothers – Andrea, who manages Lévico, and Gino, based at Jolly. Both campsites are charming. Lévico has some pitches along the lake edge and a quiet atmosphere. There is a shaded terrace for enjoying pizza and drinks in the evening. Pitches are of a good size, most grassed and well shaded with 6A electricity. Staff are welcoming and fluent in many languages including English. There is a small supermarket on site and it is a short distance to the local village. The beautiful grass shores of the lake are ideal for sunbathing and the crystal clear water is ideal for enjoying (non-motorised) water activities. This is a site where the natural beauty of an Italian lake can be enjoyed without being overwhelmed by commercial tourism. All the amenities at Camping Jolly can be enjoyed by traversing a very pretty walkway along a stream where we saw many trout.

You might like to know
Large private beach. The clear shallow waters of the lake offer opportunities for swimming, fishing, canoeing and boating. You can rent canoes and pedal boats from reception.

- ☑ Riding
- ☑ Pony trekking
- ☑ Tennis
- ☑ Sailing
- ☑ Diving
- ☑ Rafting
- ☑ Rock climbing
- ☑ Skiing *(downhill)*
- ☑ Climbing wall
- ☑ 10-pin bowling

- ☑ Yoga
- ☑ Walking tours
- ☑ Canoeing/boating
- ☑ Water skiing
- ☑ Cycling
  (road/off-road)

Facilities: Four modern sanitary blocks provide hot water for showers, washbasins and washing. Mostly British style toilets. Single locked unit for disabled visitors. Washing machines and dryer. Ironing. Freezer. Motorcaravan service point. Bar/restaurant, takeaway and good shop. Play area. Miniclub and entertainment (high season). Fishing. Satellite TV and cartoon cinema. Internet access. Kayak hire. Tennis. Torches useful. Off site: Town 2 km. with all the usual facilities and ATM. Bicycle hire 1.5 km. and bicycle track. Boat launching 500 m. Riding 3 km. Golf 7 km.

Open: 1 April - 11 October.

Directions: From the A22 Verona - Bolzano road take turn for Trento on S47 to Lévico Terme where the campsite is very well signed.
GPS: 46.00799, 11.28454

Charges guide

Per person	€ 5,00 - € 9,50
child (3-11 yrs)	€ 4,00 - € 6,00
pitch incl. electricity (6A)	€ 7,50 - € 18,00

ITALY – Pietra Ligure

Camping Dei Fiori

Viale Riviera 11, I-17027 Pietra Ligure (Ligúria)
t: 019 625 636 e: info@campingdeifiori.it
alanrogers.com/IT64040 www.campingdeifiori.it

Accommodation: ☑Pitch ☑Mobile home/chalet ☐ Hotel/B&B ☐ Apartment

This is an unsophisticated site with basic facilities situated about 500 metres from the beach. The main road runs past the entrance and the restaurant terrace is overlooked by an elevated section of this road. There are 232 pitches here, mainly seasonal for Italian campers who dominate most of the site. The 60 flat touring pitches are on the lower terrace of the site, with little shade and have a two bar fence on the lower perimeter with a four metre drop into a gulley (possibly dangerous for young children). The pitches (with 3A electricity) are difficult for manoeuvring with larger units. All food and drink is served from one small building/bar and a covered terrace across the main site road is used for eating. The site is unsuitable for young children, infirm and disabled campers.

Special offers
Book 7 days = pay only 5 days from
1/1-12/6 and from 4/9-31/12.

Book 7 days = pay only 6 days from
12/6- 26/6 and from 21/8-5/9.
Optional costs excluded

You might like to know
There is a 24 km. cycle track passing close to this site ideal for exploring the Riviera dei Fiori.

☑ Riding
☑ Pony trekking
☑ Tennis
☑ Cycling *(road)*
☑ Mountain biking
☑ Sports field
☑ Outdoor pool
☑ Sailing
☑ Windsurfing
☑ Diving

☑ Waterskiing
☑ Golf
☑ Potholing
☑ Rock climbing
☑ Hiking

Facilities: Two blocks are old and provide a mixture of British and Turkish toilets. However a new portacabin offers better showers and toilets although the majority are Turkish. Showers are token operated (20c) but hot water is solar heated and may be in short supply. The facilities are under pressure at peak times. Sinks have cold water only. Although basic facilities are provided, we would not recommend this site for disabled campers. Bar/snack bar. Takeaway (June-Sept). Shop. Swimming pool (May-Sept) and fabric paddling pool. Limited entertainment programme in season. Bicycle hire.
Off site: Beach 550 m. Riding 8 km. Golf 10 km.

Open: All year.

Directions: From the A10 take Pietra Ligure exit. Site is clearly signed 1 km. from the junction. Do not stray into town with large units – there are many restrictions and low bridges.
GPS: 44.14183, 8.27833

Charges guide

Per unit incl. 3 persons	€ 20,00 - € 36,00
extra person	€ 5,00 - € 7,00
child (4-10 yrs)	€ 3,00 - € 5,00
electricity	€ 2,00
dog	€ 2,00 - € 4,00

SLOVENIA – Bled

Camping Bled

Kidriceva 10c SI, SLO-4260 Bled
t: **045 752 000** e: **info@camping-bled.com**
alanrogers.com/SV4200 **www.camping-bled.com**

Accommodation: ☑Pitch ☑Mobile home/chalet ☐ Hotel/B&B ☐ Apartment

On the western tip of Lake Bled is Camping Bled. The waterfront here is a small public beach immediately behind which runs a gently sloping narrow wooded valley. Pitches at the front, used mainly for over-nighters, are now marked, separated by trees and enlarged, bringing the total number to 280. In areas at the back, visitors are free to pitch where they like. There is some noise coming from trains as they trundle out of a high tunnel overlooking the campsite on the line from Bled to Bohinj. But this is a small price to pay for the pleasure of being in a pleasant site from which the lake, its famous little island, its castle and its town can be explored on foot or by boat. Unlike at many other Slovenian sites the number of static units (and seasonal units) here appears to be carefully controlled, with touring caravans, motorcaravans and tents dominating.

Special offers
Free guided cycling tours. Special bird-watching and nature programmes. One hundred nesting places set up throughout the site (brochures of bird species and binoculars from reception). Free guided bird watching tour.

You might like to know
Enjoy hiking, mountain biking, water sports, rowing, fishing, paragliding, canoeing, canyoning, kayaking, climbing, horse riding, golfing, tennis and many other things. Advice, reservations and transfer arrangements at reception.

- ☑ Riding
- ☑ Pony trekking
- ☑ Crafts
- ☑ Diving
- ☑ Paintball
- ☑ Rafting
- ☑ Canyoning
- ☑ Aerial walkways
- ☑ Canoeing
- ☑ Hot air ballooning

- ☑ Birdwatching
- ☑ Paragliding
- ☑ Fishing/flyfishing
- ☑ Adventure park
- ☑ Cycling
  (road/off-road)

Facilities: Toilet facilities in five blocks are of a high standard (with free hot showers). Two blocks are heated. Solar energy used. Washing machines and dryers. Motorcaravan services. Gas supplies. Fridge hire. Supermarket. Restaurant. Play area and children's zoo. Games hall. Trampolines. Organised activities in July/Aug including children's club, excursions and sporting activities. Mountain bike tours. Live entertainment. Fishing. Bicycle hire. Internet access and WiFi. Off site: Riding 3 km. Golf 5 km. Within walking distance of waterfront and town. Restaurants nearby.

Open: 1 April - 15 October.

Directions: From the town of Bled drive along south shore of lake to its western extremity (some 2 km) to the site.
GPS: 46.36155, 14.08075

Charges guide

Per unit incl. 2 persons and electricity	€ 20,50 - € 28,50
extra person	€ 8,50 - € 12,50
child (7-13 yrs)	€ 5,95 - € 8,75
dog	€ 1,50 - € 2,50

Less 10% for stays over 6 days.

Camping Terme 3000

Kranjceva ulica 12, SLO-9226 Moravske Toplice
t: 025 121 200 e: info@terme3000.si
alanrogers.com/SV4410 www.terme3000.si

Accommodation: ☑Pitch ☑Mobile home/chalet ☐Hotel/B&B ☐Apartment

Moravske Toplice is a large site with 450 pitches. There are 250 places for touring units (all with 10A electricity), the remaining pitches being taken by seasonal campers. On a grass and gravel surface (hard tent pegs may be needed), the level, numbered pitches are of 50-80 m² There are hardstandings available in the newer area of the site. While there are a few activities on the site, it is only 200 metres from the enormous thermal spa and fun pool complex under the same name. Here there are over 5,000 m² of water activities – swimming, jet streams, water falls, water massages, four water slides (the longest is 170 m) and thermal baths. The complex also provides bars and restaurants and a large golf course. Access to the pool complex and sauna is free for campsite guests. Once you have had enough of the 22 indoor and outdoor pools, you could go walking or cycling through the surrounding woods and fields or try the delicious wines of the Goricko region.

Facilities: Modern and clean toilet facilities provide British style toilets, open washbasins and controllable, free hot showers. Laundry facilities. Football field. Tennis. Archery. Gymnastics. Daily activity programme for children (3 times a day). Off site: Large water complex with shop, bars, restaurants and takeaway. Golf.

Open: All year.

Directions: From Maribor, go east to Murska Sobota. From there go north towards Martjanci and then east towards Moravske Toplice. Access to the site is on the right before the bridge. GPS: 46.67888, 16.22165

Charges guide

Per unit incl. 2 persons and electricity € 39,00

You might like to know

'Freerider' bike centre (rent a bike service and guided bike trips).

- ☑ Riding
- ☑ Tennis
- ☑ Cycling *(road)*
- ☑ Sports field
- ☑ Outdoor pool
- ☑ Golf
- ☑ Paintball
- ☑ Hiking
- ☑ 10-pin bowling

SLOVENIA – Catez ob Savi

Camping Terme Catez

Topliska cesta 35, SLO-8251 Catez ob Savi
t: **074 936 723** e: **camp@terme-catez.si**
alanrogers.com/SV4415 www.terme-catez.si

Accommodation: ☑Pitch ☑Mobile home/chalet ☐Hotel/B&B ☐Apartment

Terme Catez is part of the modern Catez thermal spa, renowned for its medical programmes to treat rheumatism and for a wide range of programmes to improve or maintain your health. The campsite has 590 pitches, with 190 places for tourers, the remainder being taken by privately owned mobile homes and cottages. One large, open field, with some young trees – a real sun trap – provides level, grass pitches which are numbered by markings on the tarmac access roads. All have 10A electricity. It would be a very useful stop over on a journey to Croatia in the low season or for an active family holiday. The site is in the centre of a large complex which caters for most needs with its pools, large shopping centre, gym and the numerous events that are organised, such as the Magic School and Junior Olympic Games for children.

Special offers
Outdoor Olympic-size swimming pool suitable for individual and group training (open end of April until beginning of October). Campsite suitable for youth programmes. Sauna Park (eight types of sauna).

You might like to know
Winter and Summer thermal Riviera with over 12,500 m² of thermal water surface (indoor and outdoor swimming pools, water attractions, water park for children). Special preventative and rehabilitation programmes for sportsmen.

☑ Tennis
☑ Cycling *(road)*
☑ Archery
☑ Golf
☑ Paintball
☑ Kayaking
☑ Go-karting
☑ 10-pin bowling
☑ Fishing
☑ Hiking

☑ Squash
☑ Table tennis
☑ Badminton
☑ Fitness facilities

Facilities: Two modern toilet blocks with British and Turkish style toilets, open style washbasins and controllable hot showers. Facilities for disabled visitors. Laundry facilities. Motorcaravan service point. Supermarket. Kiosks for fruit, newspapers, souvenirs and tobacco. Restaurants. Bar with terrace. Several large indoor and outdoor pools (free, max. two entries per day per person). Go karts. Pedalos. Rowing boats. Jogging track. Fishing. Golf. Bicycle hire. Sauna. Solarium. Riding. Magic shows, dance nights and fashion shows organised. Casino. Video games. Off site: Golf 7 km.

Open: All year.

Directions: From Ljubljana take no. 1 road southeast towards Zagreb and follow signs for Terme Catez (close to Brezice). GPS: 45.89137, 15.62598

Charges guide

Per person	€ 14,50 - € 15,80
child (4-12 yrs)	€ 7,25 - € 7,90
electricity	€ 3,60
dog	€ 3,20

Camping Terme Ptuj

Pot v toplice 9, SLO-2251 Ptuj
t: **027 494 100** e: **info@terme-ptuj.si**
alanrogers.com/SV4440 **www.terme-ptuj.si**

Accommodation: ☑Pitch ☑Mobile home/chalet ☐Hotel/B&B ☐Apartment

Camping Terme Ptuj is close to the river, just outside the interesting town of Ptuj. It is a small site with only 100 level pitches, all for tourers and all with 10A electricity. In two areas, the pitches to the left are on part grass and part gravel hardstanding and are mainly used for motorcaravans. The pitches on the right hand side are on grass under mature trees, off a circular, gravel access road. In this area a promising new toilet block was being built when we visited. The main attraction of this site is clearly the adjacent thermal spa and fun pool complex that also attracts many local visitors. It has several slides and fun pools, as well as a sauna, solarium and spa bath. The swimming pools are free for campsite guests. This site would also be a useful stop over en-route to Croatia and the beautiful historic towns of Ptuj and Maribor are well worth a visit.

You might like to know
The thermal park has no fewer than six swimming pools and the longest water slide in Slovenia!

☑ Riding
☑ Pony trekking
☑ Tennis
☑ Cycling *(road)*
☑ Mountain biking
☑ Sports field
☑ Outdoor pool
☑ Crafts
☑ Sailing
☑ Windsurfing

☑ Golf
☑ Paintball
☑ Skiing *(downhill)*
☑ Kayaking
☑ Climbing wall

Facilities: Modern toilet block with British and Turkish style toilets, open washbasins and controllable, hot showers (free). En-suite facilities for disabled visitors with toilet and basin. Two washing machines. Football field. Torch useful. Off site: Large thermal spa 100 m. Bar/restaurant and snack bar 100 m.

Open: All year.

Directions: From Maribor go southeast towards Ptuj and follow the site signs. Site is on the left before you cross the river and not very well signed. GPS: 46.422683, 15.85495

Charges guide

Per person	€ 12,50 - € 15,50
child (7-14 yrs)	€ 8,75 - € 10,85
child (4-7 yrs)	€ 6,25 - € 7,75
electricity	€ 3,50
dog	€ 3,00

SLOVENIA – Verzej

Camping Terme Banovci

Banovci 1A, SLO-9241 Verzej
t: 2 5131400 e: terme@terme-banovci.si
alanrogers.com/SV4445 www.terme-banovci.si

Accommodation: ☑Pitch ☑Mobile home/chalet ☐ Hotel/B&B ☐ Apartment

Terme Banovci is a comfortable, quiet, countryside site with 130 normal touring pitches plus 50 FKK naturist pitches which are located separately. The grassed pitches have ample shade, are accessed by gravel roads and all have 10A electricity. Entry to the indoor 35-38°C and outdoor 25-27°C pools with a total surface area of 2,000 square metres is free to campers. The pools with large outdoor slide and ample space for sunbathing are all that one expects from a modern, well equipped, thermal spa. The comfortable restaurant is built in traditional style and drinks and food are available on the terrace beside the pool. The indoor pool contains mineral thermal water which is pumped up from a depth of 1,700 m. The water is rich in fluorides and recognised as being beneficial in treating rheumatism and other ailments. The outdoor pool is filled with normal water and is equipped with underwater massage jets, whirlpools, a waterfall and water slide. In addition there is a paddling pool for children.

You might like to know

Please note, this is partly a naturist campsite, the first in Europe to be developed around a thermal complex.

☑ Riding
☑ Tennis
☑ Cycling (road)
☑ Outdoor pool
☑ Crafts
☑ Archery
☑ Paintball
☑ Rafting
☑ Fishing

Facilities: Two well appointed heated sanitary blocks. Washbasins in cabins. Facilities for disabled people. Laundry. Motorhome service point. Nordic walking. Volleyball. Tennis. Morning gymnastics. Animation programme. Wellness centre with three Finnish saunas. Solarium. Turkish bath. Various massage programmes (at extra cost). Off site: Lots of walking and cycle paths.

Open: All year,
naturist camping 15 March - 15 November.

Directions: Site is 38 km. east of Maribor. From A5 take Vucja Vas exit and head south on the 230 for 5 km. to Knzevci pri Ljutomeru. Then turn northeast on the 439 for 1 km. and fork right to Banovci. Site is 400 m northeast of Banovci and is signed in the village.
GPS: 46.573181, 16.171494

Charges guide

Per unit incl. 2 persons and electricity	€ 27,50 - € 29,50
dog	€ 3,00

Balatontourist Camping Füred

Széchenyi ut 24, H-8230 Balatonfüred (Veszprem County)
t: 87 580 241   e: fured@balatontourist.hu
alanrogers.com/HU5090   www.balatontourist.hu

Accommodation: ☑Pitch ☑Mobile home/chalet ☐Hotel/B&B ☐Apartment

This is a large international holiday village rather than just a campsite. Pleasantly decorated with flowers and shrubs, it offers a very wide range of facilities and sporting activities. All that one could want for a family holiday can be found here. The 890 individual pitches (60-120 m²), all with electricity (6-10A), are on either side of hard access roads on which pitch numbers are painted. Many bungalows are for rent. Mature trees cover about two-thirds of the site giving shade, with the remaining area being in the open. Directly on the lake with 800 m. of access for boats and bathing, there is also a large, grassy area for relaxation, a small beach area for children and a variety of watersports. A water ski drag lift is most spectacular with its four towers erected in the lake to pull skiers around the circuit. There is a swimming pool on site with lifeguards. Along the main road that runs through the site are shops and kiosks, with the main bar/restaurant and terrace overlooking the lake.

You might like to know
Between early July and late August the campsite offers activity programmes which repeat every second week so there is always plenty to choose from.

- ☑ Riding
- ☑ Tennis
- ☑ Cycling *(road)*
- ☑ Outdoor pool
- ☑ Sailing
- ☑ Windsurfing
- ☑ Diving
- ☑ Waterskiing
- ☑ Fishing
- ☑ Free water-slide

- ☑ Trampoline
- ☑ Beach volleyball
- ☑ Table tennis

Facilities: Six fully equipped toilet blocks around the site include hot water for dishwashing and laundry. Private cabins for rent. Laundry service. Gas supplies. Numerous bars, restaurants, cafés, food bars and supermarket (all season). Stalls and kiosks with wide range of goods and souvenirs. Excellent swimming pool (1/6-31/8). Sandy beach. Large free water chute. Animation for children. Sports activities organised for adults. 6 day diving course. Sauna. Fishing. Water ski lift. Windsurf school. Sailing. Pedaloes. Play area. Bicycle hire. Tennis. Minigolf. Video games. Internet point. Dogs are not accepted. Off site: Riding 10 km.

Open: 16 April - 3 October.

Directions: Site is just south of Balatonfüred, on Balatonfüred - Tihany road and is well signed. Gates closed 13.00-15.00 except at weekends. GPS: 46.94558, 17.87710

Charges guide

Per unit incl. 2 persons and electricity	HUF 3600 - 9200
extra person	HUF 800 - 1600
child (2-14 yrs)	HUF 500 - 1200

Martfü Health & Recreation Centre

Tüzép utca, H-5435 Martfü (Jász-Nagkyun-Szolnok County)
t: **56 580531**   e: **martfu@camping.hu**
alanrogers.com/HU5255 www.martfu-turizmus.hu

Accommodation: ☑Pitch ☑Mobile home/chalet ☐Hotel/B&B ☐Apartment

The Martfü campsite is new and modern with 61 touring pitches on newly developed, grassy terrain with rubber hardstandings. Each of around 90 m² and separated by young bushes and trees, all have electricity (16/25A), waste water drainage, cable and satellite TV. There is a water tap per two pitches. There is no shade as yet, which may cause the site to become a real suntrap in summer, when temperatures may rise up to 34 degrees. A small lake and its beach on the site will cool you off. The main attraction at this site is the thermal spa (still under construction when we visited) which is said to aid people with dermal and rheumatic problems. Martfü is right on the banks of the River Tisza, which also makes it an excellent spot for those who enjoy watersports and fishing. The village of Martfü is close with numerous shops, restaurants and bars.

You might like to know

Excellent local spa and wellness centre.

- ☑ Riding
- ☑ Pony trekking
- ☑ Tennis
- ☑ Cycling *(road)*
- ☑ Mountain biking
- ☑ Sailing
- ☑ Golf
- ☑ Hiking
- ☑ Canoeing
- ☑ Fishing

Facilities: Two modern, heated toilet blocks with British style toilets, open style washbasins, and free, controllable hot showers. Children's toilet and shower. Heated baby room. En-suite facilities for disabled visitors. Laundry. Kitchen with cooking rings. Motorcaravan services. Shop for basics. Takeaway for bread and drinks. Welcoming bar with satellite TV and internet. Bowling. Library. Sauna. Jacuzzi. Playing field. Tennis. Minigolf. Fishing. Bicycle hire. Watersports. English is spoken. Off site: Fishing 50 m. Riding 5 km. Boat launching 1,5 km.

Open: All year.

Directions: Driving into Martfu from the north on the 442 road, take the first exit at the roundabout (site is signed). Continue for about 800 m. and site is signed on the right.
GPS: 47.019933, 20.268517

Charges guide

Per person	HUF 1200
child (5-14 yrs)	HUF 600
pitch	HUF 900 - 1200
electricity	HUF 250

No credit cards.

Balatontourist Camping Napfény

Halász u. 5, H-8253 Révfülöp (Veszprem County)
t: 87 563 031   e: napfeny@balatontourist.hu
alanrogers.com/HU5370   www.balatontourist.hu

Accommodation: ☑Pitch ☑Mobile home/chalet ☐ Hotel/B&B ☐ Apartment

Camping Napfény, an exceptionally good site, is designed for families with children of all ages looking for an active holiday, and has a 200 m. frontage on Lake Balaton. The site's 395 pitches vary in size (60-110 m²) and almost all have shade – very welcome during the hot Hungarian summers – and 6-10A electricity. As with most of the sites on Lake Balaton, a train line runs just outside the site boundary. There are steps to get into the lake and canoes, boats and pedaloes for hire. An extensive entertainment programme is designed for all ages and there are several bars and restaurants of various styles. There are souvenir shops and a supermarket. In fact, you need not leave the site at all during your holiday, although there are several excursions on offer, including to Budapest or to one of the many Hungarian spas, a trip on Lake Balaton or a wine tour.

You might like to know

Camping Napfény is very child friendly with plenty of activities ideal for younger guests including a new paddling pool.

☑ **Cycling** *(road)*
☑ **Sports field**
☑ **Windsurfing**
☑ **Kayaking**
☑ **Pedaloes**
☑ **Fishing**

Facilities: The three excellent sanitary blocks have toilets, washbasins (open style and in cabins) with hot and cold water, spacious showers (both preset and controllable), child size toilets and basins, and two bathrooms (hourly charge). Heated baby room. Facilities for disabled people. Launderette. Dog shower. Motorcaravan services. Supermarket. Several bars, restaurants and souvenir shops. Sports field. Tennis. Minigolf. Fishing. Bicycle hire. Canoe, rowing boats and pedalo hire. Extensive entertainment programme for all ages. Free internet access. Off site: Riding 3 km.

Open: 30 April - 30 September.

Directions: Follow road 71 from Veszprém southeast to Keszthely. Site is in Révfülöp. GPS: 46.82417, 17.63733

Charges guide

Per unit incl. 2 persons and electricity	HUF 3400 - 7150
extra person	HUF 800 - 1200
child (2-14 yrs)	HUF 550 - 900
dog	HUF 550 - 900

AUSTRIA – Natters

Ferienparadies Natterer See

Natterer See 1, A-6161 Natters (Tirol)
t: 051 254 6732 e: info@natterersee.com
alanrogers.com/AU0060 www.natterersee.com

Accommodation: ☑Pitch ☑Mobile home/chalet ☐ Hotel/B&B ☐ Apartment

In a quiet location arranged around two lakes and set amid beautiful alpine scenery, this site founded in 1930 is renowned as one of Austria's top sites. Over the last few years a lot of improvement work has been carried out and pride of place on site is a new, innovative, award-winning multifunctional building. This contains all of the sanitary facilities expected of a top site including a special children's section, private bathrooms to rent and a dog bath, plus reception, shop, café/bar/bistro and a cinema and, on the upper floor, a panorama lounge as well as a large collection of model cars. Almost all of the 235 pitches are for touring units. They are terraced, set on gravel/grass, all have electricity and most offer a splendid view of the mountains. The site's lakeside restaurant with bar and large terrace has a good menu and is the ideal place to spend the evening. With a bus every hour and the city centre only 19 minutes away this is also a good site from which to visit the city.

You might like to know
The campsite is open all year and is situated near the city of Innsbruck, a former Winter Olympic Games city.

☑ Riding
☑ Tennis
☑ Mountain biking
☑ Golf
☑ Skiing (downhill)
☑ Curling
☑ Ice skating
☑ Ice hockey
☑ Sailing boats
☑ Paragliding

Facilities: The large sanitary blocks have underfloor heating, some washbasins in cabins, plus excellent facilities for babies, children and disabled people. Laundry facilities. Motorcaravan services. Fridge box hire. Bar. Restaurant and takeaway (20/3-3/10). Pizzeria. Good shop. Playgrounds. Children's activity programme. Child minding (day nursery) in high season. Sports field. Archery. Internet point and WiFi. Open air cinema. Mountain bike hire. Aquapark (1/5-30/9). Surf bikes and pedalos. Canoes and mini sailboats for rent. Dogs are not accepted in high season (July/Aug). Off site: Tennis and minigolf nearby. Riding 6 km. Golf 12 km.

Open: All year excl. 31 October - 14 December.

Directions: From Inntal autobahn (A12) take Brenner autobahn (A13) as far as Innsbruck-sud/Natters exit (no. 3). Turn left by petrol station onto the B182 to Natters. At roundabout take first exit and immediately right again and follow signs to site 4 km. GPS: 47.23755, 11.34201

Charges guide

Per unit incl. 2 persons and electricity	€ 25,20 - € 42,00
extra person	€ 5,90 - € 8,20
child (under 13 yrs)	€ 4,60 - € 6,00
dog (excl. July/Aug)	€ 3,50 - € 4,00

Aktiv-Camping Prutz

Pontlatzstrasse 22, A-6522 Prutz (Tirol)
t: 054 722 648 e: info@aktiv-camping.at
alanrogers.com/AU0155 www.aktiv-camping.at

Accommodation: ☑Pitch ☑Mobile home/chalet ☐ Hotel/B&B ☐ Apartment

Aktiv-Camping is a long site which lies beside, and is fenced off from, the River Inn. Most of the 100 individual level pitches are for touring and range in size from 80 to 100 m² They all have 6A electrical connections and in the larger area fit together sideways and back to back. As a result, the site can sometimes have the appearance of being quite crowded. There is a separate overnight area for motorcaravans. This is an attractive area with many activities in both summer and winter for all age groups. You may well consider using this site not just as an overnight stop, but also for a longer stay. From Roman times onwards, when the Via Augusta passed through, this border region's stategic importance has left behind many fortifications that today feature among its many tourist attractions. Others include hiking, cycling and mountain biking, swimming in lakes and pools as well interesting, educational and adventurous activities for children. The Tiroler Summer card is available without charge at reception.

You might like to know
Why not hike to see the wonderful view from the Kaunertaler glacier?

☑ Riding
☑ Tennis
☑ Mountain biking
☑ Outdoor pool
☑ Rock climbing
☑ Skiing *(downhill)*
☑ Snowboarding
☑ Pedaloes
☑ Fishing
☑ Nordic walking

Facilities: The sanitary facilities are of a high standard, with private cabins and good facilities for disabled visitors. Baby room. Washing machine. Dog shower. Small shop. Bar (15/5-15/9). Takeaway (15/5-15/9). Play room. Ski room. Skating rink. Children's entertainment. Guided walks, skiing (free shuttle service). WiFi. Off site: Riding 1 km. Indoor pool at Feichten, Pilgrim's Church at Kaltenbrunn. Kaunertaler Glacier.

Open: All year.

Directions: Travelling west from Innsbruck on the E60/A12 for about 65 km. Exit at Landeck and follow the B315 (direction Reschenpass) turn south onto the B180 signed Bregenz, Arlberg, Innsbruck and Fernpass for 11 km. to Prutz. Site is signed to the right from the B180 B315 over the bridge. GPS: 47.08833, 10.65831

Charges guide

Per unit incl. 2 persons and electricity	€ 15,50 - € 25,10
extra person	€ 3,90 - € 6,90
child (5-14 yrs)	€ 2,50 - € 3,50
dog	€ 2,00 - € 3,00

Camping Grassi

CH-3714 Frutigen (Bern)
t: 033 671 1149 e: campinggrassi@bluewin.ch
alanrogers.com/CH9360 www.camping-grassi.ch

Accommodation: ☑Pitch ☑Mobile home/chalet ☐ Hotel/B&B ☐ Apartment

This is a small site with about half the pitches occupied by static caravans, used by their owners for weekends and holidays. The 70 or so places available for tourists are not marked out but it is said that the site is not allowed to become overcrowded. Most places are on level grass with two small terraces at the end of the site. There is little shade but the site is set in a river valley with trees on the hills which enclose the area. Electricity is available for all pitches but long leads may be required in parts. It would make a useful overnight stop en-route for Kandersteg and the railway station, where cars can join the train for transportation through the Lotschberg Tunnel to the Rhône Valley and Simplon Pass, or for a longer stay to explore the Bernese Oberland.

You might like to know
Some typically Tyrolean adventure sports are on offer at a nearby adventure park.

- ☑ Tennis
- ☑ Cycling (road)
- ☑ Mountain biking
- ☑ Outdoor pool
- ☑ Crafts
- ☑ Rock climbing
- ☑ Hiking
- ☑ Skiing (downhill)
- ☑ Snowboarding
- ☑ Fishing

Facilities: The well constructed, heated sanitary block is of good quality. Washing machine and dryer. Gas supplies. Motorcaravan services. Communal room with TV. Kiosk (1/7-31/8). Play area and play house. Mountain bike hire. Fishing. Bicycle hire. WiFi. Off site: Shops and restaurants 10 minutes walk away in village. Riding 2 km. Outdoor and indoor pools, tennis and minigolf in Frutigen. Skiing and walking. A new sauna and wellness centre has opened in the village.

Open: All year.

Directions: Take Kandersteg road from Spiez and leave at Frutigen Dorf exit from where site is signed. GPS: 46.58142, 7.64741

Charges guide

Per unit incl. 2 persons and electricity	CHF 20,80 - 28,80
extra person	CHF 6,40
child (1-16 yrs)	CHF 1,50 - 3,20
dog	CHF 1,50

Camping Manor Farm 1

CH-3800 Interlaken-Thunersee (Bern)
t: 033 822 2264 e: manorfarm@swisscamps.ch
alanrogers.com/CH9420 www.manorfarm.ch

Accommodation: ☑Pitch ☑Mobile home/chalet ☐ Hotel/B&B ☐ Apartment

Manor Farm has been popular with British visitors for many years, as this is one of the traditional touring areas of Switzerland. The flat terrain is divided entirely into 525 individual, numbered pitches which vary considerably both in size (60-100 m²) and price with 4/13A electricity available and shade in some places. There are 144 equipped with electricity, water, drainage and 55 also have cable TV connections. Reservations are made, although you should find space except perhaps in late July/early August, but the best places may be taken. The site lies outside the town on the northern side of the Thunersee, with most of the site between road and lake but with one part on the far side of the road. Interlaken is very much a tourist town, but the area is rich in scenery, with innumerable mountain excursions and walks available. The lakes and Jungfrau railway are near at hand. Manor Farm is a large campsite, efficiently run, with a minimum of formality and would suit those looking for an active family holiday.

You might like to know

The campsite is located on the shores of Lake Thun amid beautiful mountain scenery with many opportunities for watersports and excursions. Also open in winter.

- ☑ Riding
- ☑ Cycling *(road)*
- ☑ Outdoor pool
- ☑ Sailing
- ☑ Windsurfing
- ☑ Golf
- ☑ Hiking
- ☑ Fishing

Facilities: Eight separate toilet blocks are practical, heated and fully equipped. Twenty private toilet units are for rent. Laundry facilities. Motorcaravan services. Gas supplies. Excellent shop (1/4-15/10). Site-owned restaurant adjoining (1/3-30/11). Snack bar (July/Aug). TV room. Playground and paddling pool. Minigolf. Bicycle hire. Sailing and windsurfing school. Lake swimming. Boat hire (slipway for your own). Fishing. Daily activity and entertainment programme in high season. Excursions. Max. 1 dog. WiFi (charged). Off site: Golf 500 m. (handicap card). Riding 3 km. Good area for cycling and walking. Free bus service to heated indoor and outdoor swimming pools (free entry).

Open: All year.

Directions: Site is 3 km. west of Interlaken along the road running north of the Thunersee towards Thun. Follow signs for 'Camp 1'. From A8 (bypassing Interlaken) take exit 24 marked 'Gunten, Beatenberg', which is a spur road close to site. GPS: 46.68509, 7.81222

Charges guide

Per unit incl. 2 persons and electricity	CHF 37,00 - 63,50
extra person	CHF 10,50
child (6-15 yrs)	CHF 5,00

SWITZERLAND – Interlaken

Camping Lazy Rancho 4

Lehnweg 6, CH-3800 Interlaken (Bern)
t: **033 822 8716** e: **info@lazyrancho.ch**
alanrogers.com/CH9430 www.lazyrancho.ch

Accommodation: ☑Pitch ☑Mobile home/chalet ☐Hotel/B&B ☐Apartment

This super site is in a quiet location with fantastic views of the dramatic mountains of Eiger, Monch and Jungfrau. Neat, orderly and well maintained, the site is situated in a wide valley just 1 km. from Lake Thun and 1.5 km. from Interlaken. The English speaking owners lovingly care for the site and will endeavour to make you feel very welcome. Connected by gravel roads, the 155 pitches, of which 90 are for touring units, are on well tended level grass (some with hardstanding, all with 10A electricity). There are 28 pitches also with water and waste water drainage. This is a quiet friendly site, popular with British visitors. The owners offer advice on day trips out, and how to get the best bargains which can be had on the railway.

You might like to know

You can reach the summit of the Niesen Mountain using a funicular railway; from there you can enjoy the great views of Lake Thun and the Bernese Oberland.

- ☑ Riding
- ☑ Cycling *(road)*
- ☑ Mountain biking
- ☑ Golf
- ☑ Rafting
- ☑ Canyoning
- ☑ Rock climbing
- ☑ Fishing
- ☑ Parachuting
- ☑ Paragliding

Facilities: Two good sanitary blocks are both heated with free hot showers, good facilities for disabled customers and a baby room. Laundry. Campers' kitchen with microwave, cooker, fridge and utensils. Motorcaravan service point. Well stocked shop. Play area. Small swimming pool. Bicycle hire (June-Aug). Free WiFi. Off site: Cycle trails and way-marked footpaths. Riding 500 m. Golf and bicycle hire 1 km. Lake Thun for fishing 1.5 km. Boat launching 1.5 km. Interlaken (free regular bus service 400 m. from site) and leisure centre 2 km.

Open: 1 May - 15 October.

Directions: Site is on north side of Lake Thun. From road 8 (Thun - Interlaken) on south side of lake take exit 24 Interlaken West. Follow towards lake at roundabout then follow signs for campings. Lazy Rancho is Camp 4. The last 500 m. is a little narrow but no problem. GPS: 46.68605, 7.830633

Charges guide

Per unit incl. 2 persons and electricity	CHF 26,50 - 47,70
extra person	CHF 6,00 - 6,60
child (6-15 yrs)	CHF 3,50 - 3,80
dog	CHF 3,00

Payment also accepted in euros.

SWITZERLAND – Lauterbrunnen

Camping Jungfrau

CH-3822 Lauterbrunnen (Bern)
t: 033 856 2010 e: info@camping-jungfrau.ch
alanrogers.com/CH9460 www.camping-jungfrau.ch

Accommodation: ☑Pitch ☑Mobile home/chalet ☐ Hotel/B&B ☐ Apartment

This friendly site has a very imposing and dramatic situation in a steep valley with a fine view of the Jungfrau at the end. It is a popular site and, although you should usually find space, in season do not arrive too late in the day. A fairly extensive area with grass pitches and hardcore access roads. All 391 pitches (250 for touring) have shade in parts, electrical connections (13A) and 50 have water and drainage also. Over 30% of the pitches are taken by seasonal caravans and it is used by two tour operators. Family owned and run by Herr and Frau Fuchs, you can be sure of a warm welcome and English is spoken. You can laze here amid real mountain scenery, though it does lose the sun a little early. There are many active pursuits available in the area, as well as trips on the Jungfrau railway and mountain lifts.

You might like to know
Ski store on site and a free bus to ski resorts in the winter season.

- ☑ **Cycling** *(road)*
- ☑ **Mountain biking**
- ☑ **Sports field**
- ☑ **Rock climbing**
- ☑ **Hiking**
- ☑ **Skiing** *(downhill)*
- ☑ **Skiing** *(cross-country)*
- ☑ **Snowboarding**
- ☑ **Aerial walkways**
- ☑ **Ice skating**

Facilities: Three fully equipped modern sanitary blocks can be heated in winter and one provides facilities for disabled visitors. Baby baths. Laundry facilities. Motorcaravan services. Well equipped campers' kitchen. Excellent shop with photo printing facility. Self-service restaurant with takeaway (May-end Oct). General room with tables and chairs, TV, drink machines, amusements. Playgrounds and covered play area. Excursions and some entertainment in high season. Mountain bike hire. Internet point and WiFi. ATM. Drying room. Ski store. Off site: Free bus to ski station (in winter only).

Open: All year.

Directions: Go through Lauterbrunnen and fork right at far end (look for signpost) before road bends left, 100 m. before church. The final approach is not very wide.
GPS: 46.58807, 7.91077

Charges guide

Per person	CHF 9,80 - 11,90
child (6-15 yrs)	CHF 4,80 - 5,50
pitch incl. electricity (plus meter in winter)	CHF 22,50 - 27,00
car	CHF 3,50 - 4,00
dog	CHF 3,00

SWITZERLAND – Engelberg

Camping Eienwäldli

Wasserfallstrasse 108, CH-6390 Engelberg (Unterwalden)
t: 041 637 1949 e: info@eienwaeldli.ch
alanrogers.com/CH9570 www.eienwaeldli.ch

Accommodation: ☑Pitch ☑Mobile home/chalet ☑Hotel/B&B ☐ Apartment

This super site has facilities which must make it one of the best in Switzerland. It is situated in a beautiful location 3,500 feet above sea level, surrounded by mountains, on the edge of the delightful village of Engelberg. Half of the site is taken up by static caravans which are grouped together at one side. The camping area is in two parts – nearest the entrance there are 57 hardstandings for caravans and motorcaravans, all with electricity (metered) and beyond this is a flat meadow for about 70 tents. Reception can be found in the very modern foyer of the Eienwäldli Hotel which also houses the indoor pool, health complex, shop and café/bar. The Felsenbad spa bath includes an adventure pool, steam and relaxing grottoes, Kneipp's cure, children's pool with water slides, solarium, Finnish sauna and eucalyptus steam bath (charged for). Being about 35 km. from Luzern by road and with a rail link, it makes a quiet, peaceful base from which to explore the Vierwaldstattersee region, walk in the mountains or just enjoy the scenery. The area is famous as a winter sports region and summer tourist resort.

You might like to know
The wellness area extends over 1000 m² on three separate floors.

☑ Riding
☑ Cycling *(road)*
☑ Mountain biking
☑ Sports field
☑ Golf
☑ Rock climbing
☑ Hiking
☑ Skiing *(downhill)*
☑ Skiing
  (cross-country)

Facilities: The main toilet block, heated in cool weather, is situated at the rear of the hotel and has free hot water in washbasins (in cabins) and (on payment) showers. A new modern toilet block has been added near the top end of the site. Washing machines and dryers. Shop. Café/bar. Small lounge. Indoor pool complex. Ski facilities including a drying room. Large play area with a rafting pool fed by fresh water from the mountain stream. Torches useful. TV. WiFi. Golf. Off site: Golf driving range and 18-hole course near. Fishing and bicycle hire 1 km. Riding 2 km.

Open: All year.

Directions: From N2 Gotthard motorway, leave at exit 33 Stans-Sud and follow signs to Engelberg. Turn right at T-junction on edge of town and follow signs to 'Wasserfall' and site. GPS: 46.80940, 8.42367

Charges guide

Per person	CHF 6,00 - 9,00
child (6-15 yrs)	CHF 3,00 - 4,50
pitch incl. electricity (plus meter)	CHF 10,00 - 17,00
dog	CHF 1,30 - 2,00

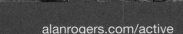

Camping Campofelice

Via alle Brere 7, CH-6598 Tenero (Ticino)
t: 091 745 1417 e: camping@campofelice.ch
alanrogers.com/CH9890 www.campofelice.ch

Accommodation: ☑Pitch ☑Mobile home/chalet ☐ Hotel/B&B ☐ Apartment

The largest site in Switzerland, it is bordered on the front by Lake Maggiore and on one side by the Verzasca estuary, where the site has its own harbour. Campofelice is divided into rows, with 860 individual pitches of average size on flat grass on either side of hard access roads. Mostly well shaded, all pitches have electricity (10-13A) and some also have water, drainage and TV connections. Pitches near the lake cost more (these are not available for motorcaravans) and a special area is reserved for small tents. English is spoken at this good, if rather expensive site. Sporting facilities are good and there are cycle paths in the area, including into Locarno. The beach by the lake is sandy, long and wider than the usual lakeside ones. It shelves gently so that bathing is safe for children.

You might like to know
There is a great sandy lakeside beach, ideal for beach volleyball.

☑ Riding
☑ Tennis
☑ Cycling *(road)*
☑ Sports field
☑ Windsurfing
☑ Waterskiing
☑ Golf
☑ Canoeing
☑ Fishing
☑ Minigolf

Facilities: The six toilet blocks (one heated) are of excellent quality. Washing machines and dryers. Motorcaravan services. Gas supplies. Supermarket, restaurant, bar and takeaway (all season). Tennis. Minigolf. Bicycle hire. Playground. Doctor calls. Dogs are not accepted Off site: Fishing 500 m. Water skiing and windsurfing 1 km. Riding 5 km. Golf 8 km.

Open: 18 March - 31 October.

Directions: On the Bellinzona - Locarno road 13, exit Tenero. Site is signed at roundabout. GPS: 46.168611, 8.855556

Charges guide

Per unit incl. 2 persons and electricity	€ 38,00 - € 82,00
extra person	€ 8,00 - € 11,00

FRANCE – Orpierre

Camping des Princes d'Orange

F-05700 Orpierre (Hautes-Alpes)
t: 04 92 66 22 53   e: campingorpierre@wanadoo.fr
alanrogers.com/FR05000   www.campingorpierre.com

Accommodation: ☑Pitch ☑Mobile home/chalet ☐Hotel/B&B ☐Apartment

This attractive, terraced site, set on a hillside above the village has been thoughtfully developed. The genuine, friendly welcome means many families return year upon year, bringing in turn new generations. Divided into five terraces, each with its own toilet block, all its 100 generously sized pitches (96 for touring units) enjoy good shade from trees and wicker canopies and have 10A electricity. In high season one terrace is reserved as a 1-star camping area for young people. Orpierre also has an enchanting maze of medieval streets and houses, almost like a trip back through the centuries. Whether you choose to drive, climb, walk or cycle, there is plenty of wonderful scenery to discover in the immediate vicinity, whilst not far away, some exhilarating hang-gliding and parascending can be enjoyed. It is renowned as a serious rock climbing venue. For those seeking to 'get away from it all' in an area of outstanding natural beauty, there can be few more tranquil sites. You will be made most welcome and will enjoy the quiet splendours the region has to offer.

Special offers
Mountain bike hire. Free guided hikes twice weekly and free mountain biking once a week in July and August.

You might like to know
The medieval village of Orpierre is surrounded by towering cliffs with over 500 possible ascents to suit all levels of climber.

☑ Riding
☑ Pony trekking
☑ Cycling *(road)*
☑ Mountain biking
☑ Outdoor pool
☑ Rafting
☑ Canyoning
☑ Rock climbing
☑ Aerial walkways
☑ Fishing

Facilities: Six well equipped toilet blocks. Baby bath. Laundry facilities. Bread. Bar (1/4-31/10). Heated swimming pool, paddling pool (15/6-15/9). Play area with small trampoline with safety net. Boules. Games room. Fridge hire. Only gas barbecues permitted. Off site: Orpierre with a few shops and bicycle hire 500 m. Fishing 7 km. Nearest shopping centre Laragne 12 km. Riding 19 km. Hang-gliding, parascending. Climbing. Gorges de Guil.

Open: 1 April - 31 October.

Directions: Turn off the N75 road at Eyguians onto the D30. The site is signed on left at crossroads in the centre of Orpierre village. GPS: 44.31121, 5.69677

Charges guide

Per unit incl. 2 persons and electricity	€ 26,30
extra person	€ 7,00
child (under 7 yrs)	€ 3,50
dog	€ 1,50

Less 25% in low season.
No credit cards.

FRANCE – Villeneuve-de-Berg

Domaine le Pommier

RN102, F-07170 Villeneuve-de-Berg (Ardèche)
t: 04 75 94 82 81   e: info@campinglepommier.com
alanrogers.com/FR07110   www.campinglepommier.com

Accommodation: ☑Pitch ☑Mobile home/chalet   ☐Hotel/B&B ☐Apartment

Domaine Le Pommier is an extremely spacious Dutch owned site of 10 hectares in 32 hectares of wooded grounds. The site is steeply terraced (a tractor is available for assistance) and has wonderful views over the Ardèche mountains and beyond. There are 423 pitches with 275 for touring units. They are grassy/stony, of good size and well spaced. Separated by young trees and hedges, some have little or no shade. All have access to electricity and water is close by. The site is not recommended for large units. Amenities include a mini-farm, including llamas, goats and ponies, and an unusual pancake restaurant. This serves an excellent range of pancakes of various flavours. The site has first class facilities, including the most up-to-date toilet blocks, a very good bar/restaurant and one of the best swimming and paddling pool complexes we have seen with two amazing new water slides – ideal for all the family.

You might like to know
The site is just 1500 metres (at an altitude of 300 metres!) from the village of Villeneuve-de-Berg with its 2500 inhabitants. The village was founded in 1284 and became famous for the cultivation of mulberry trees for silk production.

- ☑ Mountain biking
- ☑ Sports field
- ☑ Archery
- ☑ Canyoning
- ☑ Potholing
- ☑ Rock climbing
- ☑ Hiking
- ☑ Canoeing
- ☑ Water games
- ☑ Orienteering

Facilities: Four excellent toilet blocks, one with under-floor heating, provide all the necessary facilities. Comprehensive shop. Bar/restaurant. Swimming pool complex with slides (two new), paddling pools, etc. Everything opens all season. Boules. Minigolf. Activities including games in the woods, archery, water polo and tug-of-war. Bridge and water colour classes. Tennis. Soundproofed disco. Very extensive programme of events on and off site. Low season excursions. Off site: Villeneuve-de-Berg 1.5 km. River Ardèche 12 km. Potholing, rock climbing, canoeing, canyoning, mountain biking, walking and riding.

Open: 30 April - 18 September.

Directions: Site is west of Montélimar on the N102. The entrance is adjacent to the roundabout at the eastern end of the Villeneuve-de-Berg bypass. GPS: 44.57250, 4.51115

Charges guide

Per unit incl. 2 persons and electricity	€ 21,50 - € 35,50
extra person	€ 4,50 - € 7,00
child (2-4 yrs)	€ 2,50 - € 5,00
dog	free - € 4,00

Max. 6 persons per pitch.

FRANCE – La Bastide-de-Sérou

Camping l'Arize

Lieu-dit Bourtol, F-09240 La Bastide-de-Sérou (Ariège)
t: 05 61 65 81 51   e: camparize@aol.com
alanrogers.com/FR09020   www.camping-arize.com

Accommodation: ☑Pitch ☑Mobile home/chalet ☐ Hotel/B&B ☐ Apartment

The site sits in a delightful, tranquil valley among the foothills of the Pyrénées and is just east of the interesting village of La Bastide-de-Sérou, beside the River Arize (good trout fishing). The river is fenced for the safety of children on the site, but may be accessed just outside the gate. The 70 large pitches are neatly laid out on level grass within the spacious site. All have 3/6A electricity and are separated into bays by hedges and young trees. An extension to the site gives 24 large, fully serviced pitches (10A) and a small toilet block. You will receive a warm welcome from Dominique and Brigitte at this friendly little family site, and Brigitte speaks excellent English. Discounts have been negotiated for several of the local attractions (details are provided in the comprehensive pack provided on arrival – in your own language). This is a comfortable and relaxing base for touring this beautiful part of the Pyrénées, with easy access to the medieval town of Foix and even Andorra for duty-free shopping. Deer and wild boar are common in this area and may be sighted in quieter periods.

Special offers
Special golf discounts and special rates for canyoning.

You might like to know
There are over 100 km. of waymarked trails within easy reach from the site.

☑ Riding
☑ Pony trekking
☑ Tennis
☑ Cycling *(road)*
☑ Mountain biking
☑ Outdoor pool
☑ Golf
☑ Paintball
☑ Rafting
☑ Hiking

☑ Kayaking
☑ Fitness/gym
☑ 10-pin bowling
☑ Fishing

Facilities: Toilet block includes facilities for babies and disabled visitors. Laundry room. Motorcaravan services. Small swimming pool and sunbathing area. Entertainment in high season. Weekly barbecues and welcome drinks on Sundays. Fishing, riding and bicycle hire. WiFi. Off site: Several restaurants and shops within a few minutes drive. The nearest restaurant is located at the national stud for the famous Merens horses just 200 m. away and will deliver takeaway meals to your pitch. Golf 5 km.

Open: 12 March - 10 November.

Directions: Site is southeast of the village La Bastide-de-Sérou. Take the D15 towards Nescus and site is on right after about 1 km. GPS: 43.00182, 1.44538

Charges guide

Per unit incl. 2 persons and electricity	€ 16,40 - € 24,70
extra person	€ 4,00 - € 5,40
child (0-7 yrs)	€ 3,00 - € 3,60
dog	€ 1,00 - € 1,80

Discounts for longer stays in mid and low seasons.

FRANCE – Le Trein d'Ustou

Camping le Montagnou

Route de Guzet, F-09140 Le Trein d'Ustou (Ariège)
t: 05 61 66 94 97 e: campinglemontagnou@wanadoo.fr
alanrogers.com/FR09030 www.lemontagnou.com

Accommodation: ☑Pitch ☑Mobile home/chalet ☐ Hotel/B&B ☐ Apartment

The road going south out of St Girons appears to lead to nowhere other than Guzet, but it is a 30 km. (each way) detour over fairly easy roads to the little village of Le Trein d'Ustou, which is 12 km. from the up and coming winter sports resort of Guzet. Just before Le Trein d'Ustou you will find Le Montagnou, a small campsite nestling among the lush lower slopes of the mountains. It is a quiet base for winter sports activities or for touring this lovely area, with 60 level pitches on grass (48 for touring units), 30 with electricity (6, 10 or 16A). Robert and Daniele created this charming site from the forest and opened for the first time in 1996. At a lower level there is an area of the river running alongside the site which the locals use for swimming, but really the attraction here is the surrounding mountains which offer excellent winter sports facilities which include a ski-lift (10 minutes drive) and no less than 24 pistes! There are also many places of interest which Robert, who doubles as the local Director of Tourism, will be pleased to tell you about and brief you on the local wildlife.

You might like to know
The area offers a vast range of natural, cultural and heritage activities. It is 10 km. from the small village of Seix which has a supermarket, baker, butcher and restaurants.

- ☑ Riding
- ☑ Cycling *(road)*
- ☑ Mountain biking
- ☑ Outdoor pool
- ☑ Rafting
- ☑ Hiking
- ☑ Skiing *(downhill)*
- ☑ Snowboarding
- ☑ Kayaking
- ☑ Fishing

- ☑ Canyoning
- ☑ Aerial Walkways
- ☑ Parapente
- ☑ Snowshoe walks
- ☑ Geocaching

Facilities: Two toilet blocks (the second still unfinished when we visited and not in use) can be heated and include washbasins in cabins, covered dishwashing and laundry sinks, washing machine and dryers, and good facilities for disabled visitors. Snack bar with takeaway (July/Aug). Gas supplies. Baker calls every other day. Library (some English books). Fishing. Off site: Restaurant 50 m. in the village. Shops at Seix. Riding 15 km.

Open: All year.

Directions: From the A64 take D117 to St Girons. Take the D618 south towards Oust and Guzet and 3 km. north of Guzet turn right onto D3 passing Oust and Seix. At Pont de la Taule turn left on D8 for 7 km. to Trein d'Ustou. Site is on left before village.
GPS: 42.811238, 1.255381

Charges guide

Per unit incl. 2 persons and electricity	€ 15,00 - € 16,50

No credit cards.

FRANCE – Tarascon-sur-Ariege

Kawan Village le Pré Lombard

F-09400 Tarascon-sur-Ariege (Ariège)
t: 05 61 05 61 94   e: leprelombard@wanadoo.fr
alanrogers.com/FR09060   www.prelombard.com

Accommodation: ☑Pitch ☑Mobile home/chalet ☐ Hotel/B&B ☐ Apartment

This busy, good value site is located beside the attractive river Ariège near the town.
There are 180 level, grassy, pitches with shade provided by a variety of trees (electricity
10A). At the rear of the site are 70 site-owned chalets and mobile homes. A gate in the
fence provides access to the river bank for fishing. Open for a long season, it is an
excellent choice for early or late breaks, or as a stop-over en-route to the winter sun
destinations in Spain. This region of Ariège is in the foothills of the Pyrénées and 85 km.
from Andorra. Didier Mioni, the manager here follows the town motto 'S'y passos,
y demoros' – 'if you wish to come here, you will stay here' in his aim to ensure your
satisfaction on his site. At Tarascon itself you can visit the Parc Pyrénéen de l'Art
Préhistorique to view prehistoric rock paintings, or the really adventurous can take to
the air for paragliding, hang-gliding, or micro-lighting.

Special offers
Free quality sports activities for all with
sports organisers on site. Themed outings
with guide/interpreter organised by the site
(Transhumance, Airbus-Toulouse, the historical
city-centre of Carcassonne...)

You might like to know
Numerous cultural sites nearby include Grotte
de Niaux (prehistoric cave) and Château de
Montségur (Cathar site). Many free festivities
at Tarascon-sur- Ariège. Cycle track (800 m)
to Tarascon and its services.

☑ Mountain biking
☑ Outdoor pool
☑ Waterskiing
☑ Canyoning
☑ Potholing
☑ Rock climbing
☑ Aerial walkways
☑ Canoeing
☑ Sports area
☑ Fishing

☑ Parapente
☑ Via Ferrata
☑ Acrobranch Park
☑ Excursions

Facilities: Five toilet blocks of varying age,
facilities for disabled people. Laundry.
Motorcaravan services. Bar and takeaway. Shop.
Restaurant, entertainment, dancing (15/5-30/9).
Heated swimming pool (15/5-30/9). Playgrounds
for toddlers and older children. Video games
machines. Boules. Multisport court. Fishing.
Internet and WiFi on payment. Satellite TV.
Entertainment (high season), nightclub, children's
club, sports tournaments. Activity programmes
for small groups. Off site: Supermarket 300 m.
Town 600 m. Archery, kayaking and fishing
nearby. Riding 5 km. Golf 30 km. Skiing 20 km.

Open: 27 March - 13 November.

Directions: Site is 600 m. south of town,
adjacent to the river. From north, turn off main
N20 into the town, site well signed. From south
(Andorra) site signed at roundabout on town
approach. GPS: 42.83985, 1.612

Charges guide

Per unit incl. 2 persons and 10A electricity	€ 15,00 - € 32,00
extra person	€ 4,00 - € 8,00
child (2-7 yrs)	free - € 6,50
dog	free - € 2,50

Camping Ascou la Forge

F-09110 Ascou (Ariège)
t: **05 61 64 60 03** e: **info@ascou-la-forge.fr**
alanrogers.com/FR09120 www.ascou-la-forge.fr

Accommodation: ☑Pitch ☑Mobile home/chalet ☐ Hotel/B&B ☐ Apartment

The Dutch owners of Ascou La Forge will give you a warm, friendly welcome at their oasis in the mountains of the Pyrenees, close to the borders of Andorra and Spain. The site is 3,500 feet above sea level but is easily accessible for motorhomes and caravans. Lying alongside the Lauze river, there are 50 pitches. In low season, 44 mainly level, grass touring pitches with electricity are available, but this number reduces to 20 in July and August to allow more room for the large influx of campers with tents. There are also two chalets and one apartment available to rent. The site is quite open but a few trees scattered around provide some shade. The mountain views from the site are outstanding and it is an ideal base for mountain walks and various outdoor sports. It is a perfect location for people who enjoy the tranquillity of the countryside, although there is free WiFi for those that must stay in touch. Social activities (at a small extra cost) are provided and include local wine and cheese evenings, pizza evenings and barbecues.

Special offers
There are English speaking guides for hiking tours in the mountains. Free advice for multi-day hiking tours and other outdoor sports. GPS lessons. Mountain bike hire. Maps and guides for sale.

You might like to know
Many outdoor activities are organised at all levels and for all ages. Enthusiastic English speaking instructors. Many opportunities for individual sporting activities. Information available on site.

☑ **Cycling** (road)
☑ **Mountain biking**
☑ **Outdoor pool**
☑ **Rock climbing**
☑ **Hiking**
☑ **Skiing** (downhill)
☑ **Skiing** (cross-country)
☑ **Kayaking**
☑ **Fishing**
☑ **Via Ferrata**

☑ **Rafting**
☑ **Canyoning**
☑ **Speleology**
☑ **Horse riding**

Facilities: Modern, bright, sanitary block is fully equipped including facilities for disabled visitors which double as a family shower room with a baby bath. Shop. Bar with large screen for major sports events and films about the local flora and fauna. Play area. Maps and walking routes are available from reception. Free WiFi. Off site: Restaurant adjacent (all year). Bars, restaurants and shops in Ax-les-Thermes 7 km.

Open: All year.

Directions: From Ax-Les-Thermes take the D613 signed Quérigat, Quillan and Ascou-Pailhéres. After 3.6 km. turn right on D25 to site on right after 3.4 km. GPS: 42.72444, 1.89274

Charges guide

Per unit incl. 2 persons and electricity	€ 15,00 - € 23,00
extra person	€ 3,50 - € 5,00
child (0-7 yrs)	€ 2,50 - € 3,50
dog	€ 1,00 - € 1,50

FRANCE – Narbonne

Kawan Village les Mimosas

Chaussée de Mandirac, F-11100 Narbonne (Aude)
t: 04 68 49 03 72 e: info@lesmimosas.com
alanrogers.com/FR11070 www.lesmimosas.com

Accommodation: ☑Pitch ☑Mobile home/chalet ☐ Hotel/B&B ☐ Apartment

Six kilometres inland from the beaches of Narbonne and Gruissan, this site benefits from a less hectic situation than others by the sea. The site is lively with plenty to amuse and entertain the younger generation whilst offering facilities for the whole family. A free club card is needed in July/August to use the children's club, gym, sauna, tennis, minigolf, billiards etc. There are 250 pitches, 150 for touring, many in a circular layout of very good size, most with electricity (6A). There are a few 'grand confort', with reasonable shade, mostly from 2 m. high hedges. There is also a number of mobile homes and chalets to rent. This could be a very useful site offering many possibilities to meet a variety of needs; on-site entertainment (including an evening on Cathar history), and easy access to popular beaches. Nearby Gruissan is a fascinating village with its wooden houses on stilts, beaches, ruined castle, port and salt beds. Narbonne has Roman remains and inland Cathar castles are to be found perched on rugged hill tops.

Special offers
Why not take advantage of a low season holiday here? Great weather and discounted rates.

You might like to know
Discover the charms of the Mediterranean with a wide range of activities available.

☑ Pony trekking
☑ Surfing
☑ Windsurfing
☑ Kitesurfing
☑ Diving
☑ Waterskiing
☑ Paintball
☑ Canoeing
☑ Go-karting
☑ 10-pin bowling

Facilities: Sanitary buildings refurbished to a high standard. Washing machines. Shop and 'Auberge' restaurant (open all season). Takeaway. Bar. Small lounge, amusements (July/Aug). Landscaped heated pool with slides and islands (open 1/5), plus the original pool and children's pool (high season). New play area. Minigolf. Mountain bike hire. Tennis. Sauna, gym. Children's activities, sports, entertainment (high season). Bicycle hire. Multisports ground. Off site: Riding. Windsurfing/sailing school 300 m. Gruissan's beach 10 minutes. Lagoon, boating and fishing via footpath (200 m).

Open: 27 March - 1 November.

Directions: From A9 exit 38 (Narbonne-Sud) take last exit on roundabout, back over the autoroute (site signed from here). Follow signs for La Nautique and then Mandirac and site (6 km. from autoroute). Also signed from Narbonne centre. GPS: 43.13662, 3.02562

Charges guide

Per unit incl. 2 persons and electricity	€ 17,50 - € 33,00
incl. water and drain	€ 21,70 - € 38,00
extra person	€ 4,10 - € 10,00

FRANCE – La Brée-les-Bains

Camping Antioche d'Oléron

Route de Proires, F-17840 La Brée-les-Bains (Charente-Maritime)
t: 05 46 47 92 00 e: info@camping-antiochedoleron.com
alanrogers.com/FR17570 www.camping-antiochedoleron.com

Accommodation: ☑Pitch ☑Mobile home/chalet ☐ Hotel/B&B ☐ Apartment

Situated to the northeast of the island, Camping Antioche is quietly located within a five minute walk to the beach. There are 130 pitches, of which 73 are occupied by mobile homes and 57 are for touring units. The pitches are set amongst attractive shrubs and palm trees and all have electricity (10A), water and a drain. A new pool area which comprises two swimming pools (heated), two jacuzzi, two paddling pools and a raised sunbathing deck, is beautifully landscaped with palms and flowers. A small bar, restaurant and takeaway offer reasonably priced food and drinks. The site becomes livelier in season with regular evening entertainment and activities for all the family. With specially prepared trails for cycling, oyster farms and salt flats to visit, the Ile d'Oléron offers something for everyone. Bresnais market, selling local produce and products, is within easy access on foot and is held daily in high season.

You might like to know

There are popular boat trips to the off-shore Fort Boyard and to the neighbouring islands of Aix and Ré.

☑ Riding
☑ Cycling *(road)*
☑ Outdoor pool
☑ Crafts
☑ Sailing
☑ Surfing
☑ Windsurfing
☑ Golf
☑ Kayaking
☑ Fishing

Facilities: The single sanitary block is of a good standard and is kept clean and fresh. Facilities for disabled visitors. Laundry. Motorcaravan services. Bar, restaurant and snack bar (weekends only May and June, daily July/Aug). Swimming and paddling pools. Games room. Play area. WiFi. Bicycle hire (July/Aug). Off site: Beach 150 m. Fishing 150 m. Riding 1.5 km. Golf 7 km.

Open: 1 April - 30 September.

Directions: Cross the bridge on the D26 and join the D734. After St Georges turn right onto the D273E1 towards La Bree-les-Baines. At T-junction turn left from where the campsite is signed. GPS: 46.02007, -1.35764

Charges guide

Per unit incl. 2 persons and electricity	€ 21,15 - € 35,15
extra person	€ 7,10
child (1-14 yrs)	€ 3,70
dog	€ 4,00

FRANCE – Montignac

Camping le Paradis

Saint Léon-sur-Vézère, F-24290 Montignac (Dordogne)
t: 05 53 50 72 64   e: le-paradis@perigord.com
alanrogers.com/FR24060   www.le-paradis.fr

Accommodation: ☑Pitch ☑Mobile home/chalet   ☐ Hotel/B&B ☐ Apartment

Le Paradis is a well kept riverside site, halfway between Les Eyzies and Montignac. The site is very well kept and landscaped with a variety of mature shrubs and trees. The gardens are beautifully maintained which gives a wonderful sense of tranquillity. It is very easy to relax on this ecologically friendly, site. This is a family run site and you are guaranteed a warm and friendly welcome. There are 200 good sized pitches, with 27 for mobile homes to rent. The pitches are level and with easy access, all with 10A electricity, water and drainage. There are some special pitches for motorcaravans. An excellent restaurant offers a good menu, reasonably priced and using fresh local produce. The terraced area outside, makes for a convivial, family atmosphere. There are many sport and leisure activities. Direct access to the Vézère river is possible at one end of the site for canoeing and swimming. Games, competitions and evening events are aimed at maintaining a true French flavour. English is spoken. This is a site of real quality, which we thoroughly recommend.

You might like to know

The Vézère Valley with its troglodyte villages and the famous Lascaux Caves and the nearby Dordogne Valley with its castles and medieval towns offer wonderful opportunities for walkers and cyclists.

☑ Riding
☑ Pony trekking
☑ Tennis
☑ Mountain biking
☑ Sports field
☑ Outdoor pool
☑ Aerial walkways
☑ Canoeing
☑ Kayaking
☑ Fishing

Facilities: High quality, well equipped, heated toilet blocks are kept very clean. Well stocked shop (with gas). Good restaurant, takeaway. Good pool complex heated in low season, paddling pool. Play area. Tennis. BMX track. Multisport court. Canoe hire. Fishing. Bicycle hire. Quad bike and horse riding excursions. WiFi throughout. Large units are accepted by arrangement. Mobile homes to rent (no smoking) including one for visitors with disabilities (no dogs permitted). Off site: Riding 3 km.

Open: 1 April - 19 October.

Directions: Site is 12 km. north of Les Eyzies and 3 km. south of St Léon-sur-Vézère, on the east side of the D706. GPS: 45.00207, 1.0711

Charges guide

Per unit incl. 2 persons and electricity	€ 21,60 - € 30,50
extra person	€ 5,40 - € 7,40
child (3-12 yrs)	€ 4,40 - € 6,40
dog	€ 2,00

Low season reductions.
10% discount for pensioners in low season.

FRANCE – Locunolé

Castel Camping le Ty-Nadan

Route d'Arzano, F-29310 Locunolé (Finistère)
t: 02 98 71 75 47   e: infos@camping-ty-nadan.fr
alanrogers.com/FR29010   www.camping-ty-nadan.fr

Accommodation: ☑Pitch ☑Mobile home/chalet ☐Hotel/B&B ☐Apartment

Ty-Nadan is a well organised site set amongst wooded countryside along the bank of the River Elle. There are 183 grassy pitches for touring units, many with shade and 99 fully serviced. The pool complex with slides and paddling pool is very popular as are the large indoor pool complex and indoor games area with a climbing wall. There is also an adventure play park and a 'Minikids' park for 5-8 year olds, not to mention tennis courts, table tennis, pool tables, archery and trampolines. This is a wonderful site for families with children. Several tour operators use the site. An exciting and varied programme of activities is offered throughout the season – canoe and sea kayaking expeditions, rock climbing, mountain biking, aquagym, paintball, horse riding or walking – all supervised by qualified staff. A full programme of entertainment for all ages is provided in high season including concerts, Breton evenings with pig roasts, dancing, etc. (be warned, you will be actively encouraged to join in!)

You might like to know
All the on-site activities are led by fully qualified staff. Great opportunities too for fishing, cycling and mountain biking.

☑ Riding
☑ Pony trekking
☑ Tennis
☑ Archery
☑ Paintball
☑ Rock climbing
☑ Zip wires
☑ Canoeing
☑ Kayaking
☑ Climbing wall

☑ Quad bikes
☑ Adventure park

Facilities: Two older, split-level toilet blocks are of fair quality and include washbasins in cabins and baby rooms. A newer block provides easier access for disabled people. Washing machines and dryers. Restaurant, takeaway, bar and well stocked shop. Heated outdoor pool (17x8 m). Indoor pool. Small river beach (unfenced). Indoor badminton and rock climbing facility. Activity and entertainment programmes (all season). Horse riding centre. Bicycle hire. Boat hire. Canoe trips. Fishing. Internet access and WiFi (charged). Off site: Beaches 20 minutes by car. Golf 12 km.

Open: 27 March - 2 September.

Directions: Make for Arzano which is northeast of Quimperlé on the Pontivy road and turn off D22 just west of village at site sign. Site is about 3 km. GPS: 47.90468, -3.47477

Charges guide

Per unit incl. 2 persons and electricity	€ 20,80 - € 47,80
extra person	€ 4,50 - € 9,10
child (2-6 yrs)	€ 1,90 - € 5,60
dog	€ 1,90 - € 6,00

Airotel Camping la Côte d'Argent

F-33990 Hourtin-Plage (Gironde)
t: 05 56 09 10 25   e: info@cca33.com
alanrogers.com/FR33110   www.cca33.com

Accommodation: ☑Pitch ☑Mobile home/chalet ☑Hotel/B&B ☐ Apartment

Côte d'Argent is a large, well equipped site for leisurely family holidays. It makes an ideal base for walkers and cyclists with over 100 km. of cycle lanes in the area. Hourtin-Plage is a pleasant, invigorating resort on the Atlantic coast and a popular location for watersports enthusiasts, The site's top attraction is its pool complex where wooden bridges connect the pools and islands and there are sunbathing and play areas plus an indoor heated pool. The site has 588 touring pitches (all with 10A electricity), not clearly defined, arranged under trees with some on soft sand. Entertainment takes place at the bar near the entrance (until 00.30). Spread over 20 hectares of undulating sand-based terrain and in the midst of a pine forest. There are 48 hardstandings for motorcaravans outside the site, providing a cheap stopover, but with no access to site facilities. The site is well organised and ideal for children.

Special offers
Free activities in July/August: children's club (6-11 yrs), evening entertainment, sporting and other activities.

You might like to know
Large aquatic complex 3500 m² with covered, heated pool. Multisport court. Activity Centre with shops, games room, cycle hire, video games and fitness room.

- ☑ Riding
- ☑ Pony trekking
- ☑ Tennis
- ☑ Crafts
- ☑ Archery
- ☑ Waterskiing
- ☑ Aerial walkways
- ☑ Kayaking
- ☑ Pedaloes
- ☑ Fishing

- ☑ Play area
- ☑ Teenagers' games
- ☑ Sailing & surfing
- ☑ Canoeing & boating

Facilities: Very clean sanitary blocks include provision for disabled visitors. Washing machines. Motorcaravan service points. Large supermarket, restaurant, takeaway, pizzeria bar (all open 1/6-15/9). Four outdoor pools with slides and flumes (1/6-19/9). Indoor pool (all season). Massage (Institut de Beauté). Tennis. Play areas. Miniclub, organised entertainment in season. Bicycle hire. Internet. ATM. Charcoal barbecues are not permitted. Hotel (12 rooms). Off site: Path to the beach 300 m. Fishing and riding. Golf 30 km.

Open: 12 May - 19 September.

Directions: Turn off the D101 Hourtin - Soulac road 3 km. north of Hourtin. Then join the D101E signed Hourtin-Plage. Site is 300 m. from the beach. GPS: 45.22297, -1.16465

Charges guide

Per unit incl. 2 persons and electricity	€ 24,00 - € 52,00
extra person	€ 3,00 - € 7,50
child (3-9 yrs)	€ 2,50 - € 6,50
dog	€ 2,00 - € 5,50

Camping le Tedey

Par le Moutchic, route de Longarisse, F-33680 Lacanau-Lac (Gironde)
t: **05 56 03 00 15** e: **camping@le-tedey.com**
alanrogers.com/FR33290 www.le-tedey.com

Accommodation: ☑Pitch ☑Mobile home/chalet ☐ Hotel/B&B ☐ Apartment

With direct access to a large lake and beach, this site enjoys a beautiful tranquil position set in an area of 14 hectares amidst mature pine trees. There are 700 pitches of which 670 are for touring units with just 30 mobile homes and chalets available for rent. The pitches are generally level and grassy although the site is on a slope. Dappled sunlight shines through the trees. Electricity is available to all pitches and 223 also have water and waste water drainage. The bar is close to the lake with a large indoor and outdoor seating area. The owners and staff are friendly and helpful and English is spoken. There is an open air cinema on Saturdays and Wednesdays as well as other entertainment in July and August. A children's club is also organised. The takeaway sells a variety of food and the shop next door is well stocked. This is an attractive well maintained site where you get a feeling of space and calm. There are many places of interest nearby and it is a short drive to Bordeaux.

You might like to know

Why not visit the great city of Bordeaux? It is less than one hour away.

☑ Riding
☑ Cycling *(road)*
☑ Mountain biking
☑ Sailing
☑ Windsurfing
☑ Golf
☑ Hiking
☑ Canoeing
☑ Pedaloes
☑ Fishing

Facilities: Four modern sanitary blocks with facilities for disabled visitors and babies. Laundry facilities. Bar with terrace. Crêperie. Takeaway. Bicycle hire. Boating on the lake. Pétanque. Playground. Gas barbecues only on pitches. Dogs are not accepted in July/Aug. Internet access. Off site: Surfing. Riding. Golf. Cycling.

Open: 28 April - 19 September.

Directions: From Lacanau take the D6 to Lacanau-Océan. Take Route de Longarisse and camping is well signed.
GPS: 44.98620, -1.13410

Charges guide

Per unit incl. 2 persons and electricity	€ 20,50 - € 26,00
extra person	€ 3,30 - € 6,00
child (2-10 yrs)	€ 2,75 - € 3,40

Leading Camping les Alicourts

Domaine des Alicourts, F-41300 Pierrefitte-sur-Sauldre (Loir-et-Cher)
t: **02 54 88 63 34** e: **info@lesalicourts.com**
alanrogers.com/FR41030 www.lesalicourts.com

Accommodation: ☑Pitch ☑Mobile home/chalet ☐ Hotel/B&B ☐ Apartment

A secluded holiday village set in the heart of the forest and with many sporting facilities and a super spa centre, Parc des Alicourts is midway between Orléans and Bourges, to the east of the A71. There are 490 pitches, 150 for touring and the remainder occupied by mobile homes and chalets. All pitches have electricity connections (6A) and good provision for water, and most are 150 m². Locations vary from wooded to more open areas, thus giving a choice of amount of shade. All facilities are open all season and the leisure amenities are exceptional. The Senséo Balnéo centre offers indoor pools, hydrotherapy, massage and spa treatments for over 18s only (some special family sessions are provided). An inviting outdoor water complex (all season) includes two swimming pools, a pool with wave machine and a beach area, not forgetting three water slides. Competitions and activities are organised including a high season club for children with an entertainer twice a day, a disco once a week and a dance for adults. Member of Leading Campings Group.

Special offers
Family activity passes available.
Numerous free activities.

You might like to know
All activities available from the day the site is open until the day it is closed.

☑ **Pony trekking**
☑ **Tennis**
☑ **Cycling** *(road)*
☑ **Outdoor pool**
☑ **Archery**
☑ **Golf**
☑ **Pedaloes**
☑ **Fitness/gym**
☑ **Go-karting**
☑ **Fishing**

☑ **Canoeing**
☑ **Sports field**
☑ **Mini-disc golf**
☑ **Minigolf**
☑ **Rambling**

Facilities: Three modern sanitary blocks include some washbasins in cabins and baby bathrooms. Laundry facilities. Facilities for disabled visitors. Motorcaravan services. Shop. Restaurant. Takeaway in bar with terrace. Pool complex. Spa centre. 7 hectare lake (fishing, bathing, canoes, pedaloes). 9-hole golf course. Adventure play area. Tennis. Minigolf. Boules. Roller skating/skateboarding (bring own equipment). Bicycle hire. Internet access and WiFi (charged).

Open: 29 April - 9 September.

Directions: From A71, take Lamotte Beuvron exit (no 3) or from N20 Orléans to Vierzon turn left on to D923 towards Aubigny. After 14 km. turn right at camping sign on to D24E. Site is signed in 4 km. GPS: 47.54398, 2.19193

Charges guide

Per unit incl. 2 persons and electricity	€ 19,00 - € 42,00
extra person	€ 7,00 - € 10,00
child (7-17 yrs)	€ 5,00 - € 8,00
child (1-6 yrs)	free - € 6,00
dog	€ 5,00 - € 7,00

FRANCE – Agos-Vidalos

Camping Soleil du Pibeste

16 avenue du Lavedan, F-65400 Agos-Vidalos (Hautes-Pyrénées)
t: **05 62 97 53 23** e: **info@campingpibeste.com**
alanrogers.com/FR65090 www.campingpibeste.com

Accommodation: ☑Pitch ☑Mobile home/chalet ☐Hotel/B&B ☐Apartment

Soleil du Pibeste is a quiet, rural site with well tended grass and flower beds. It has 38 touring pitches, all with electricity (3-15A) and some shade. The Dusserm family welcomes all arrivals with a drink, and the friendly reception has an area for local foods, maps and good tourist information. This site is special because of the range and type of activities which it offers. These include tai chi, qi gong, massage, archery, walking, climbing and canoeing. Choral and creative activities are offered. The swimming pool is on a terrace above the pitches. It has sunbeds, a paddling pool and waterfall and the most magnificent mountain views. Ongoing improvements include a second swimming pool, incorporating facilities for those with disabilities. There is no shop for basic needs, though the supermarket is fairly easily accessed. The bar and restaurant area is large and well-equipped. The site has a bus stop just outside, providing access to Argeles-Gazost and the renowned pilgrimage town of Lourdes. The family also offers a pick up service from various airports and towns.

Special offers
Inclusive packages with accommodation rental plus activities – build your own daily programme. Fully qualified instructors – safety always top priority.

You might like to know
Various courses on offer with qualified instructors.

☑ Riding
☑ Pony trekking
☑ Tennis
☑ Archery
☑ Rafting
☑ Canyoning
☑ Potholing
☑ Rock climbing
☑ Aerial walkways
☑ Climbing wall

☑ Roller skating
☑ Tai chi - Qi gong
☑ Creative crafts
☑ Skiing/winter sports
☑ Canoeing/boating

Facilities: Two heated toilet blocks. Baby room. Facilities for disabled visitors (key). Cleaning can be variable. Washing machine, dryer. Motorcaravan services. Bar, snacks, piano, internet. Room for playing cards or reading. Swimming, paddling pools. Small play area. Boules, archery, basketball, volleyball. Table tennis. Bicycle hire. Tai Chi and other relaxation classes. Off site: Fishing 800 m. Rafting 2 km. Skiing 2 km. Golf 10 km. Riding 15 km.

Open: 1 May - 30 September.

Directions: Agos Vidalos is on the N21, which becomes the D821, 5 km. south of Lourdes. Leave express-way at second exit, signed Agos Vidalos and continue on D921B to site, a short distance on the right. GPS: 43.03557, -0.07093

Charges guide

Per unit incl. 2 persons and electricity	€ 25,00 - € 34,00
extra person	€ 8,00
dog	€ 5,00

FRNACE – Argelès-sur-Mer

Camping la Sirène

Route de Taxo á la Mer, F-66702 Argelès-sur-Mer (Pyrénées-Orientales)
t: 04 68 81 04 61   e: contact@camping-lasirene.fr
alanrogers.com/FR66560   www.camping-lasirene.fr

Accommodation: ☑Pitch ☑Mobile home/chalet ☐Hotel/B&B ☐Apartment

From the moment you step into the hotel-like reception area you realise that this large site offers the holiday maker everything they could want in a well managed and convenient location close to Argelès-sur-Mer and the beaches. The 740 mobile homes and chalets vary in standard but all are less than five years old, very clean, comfortable and located on neat tidy pitches. There are also some touring pitches. In the summer there are 170 staff on duty to ensure your stay is as enjoyable as they can make it. All the shops and amenities are near reception making the accommodation areas quite peaceful and relaxing. There are many things to do and summer visitors have the option of using the free bus service to the beach where the site has its own club where you can even go windsurfing at no charge.

You might like to know
There is a PADI and CMAS certificated diving centre here. Beginners and experts are all welcome at this excellent centre.

☑ Tennis
☑ Mountain biking
☑ Sports field
☑ Archery
☑ Sailing
☑ Windsurfing
☑ Diving
☑ Hiking
☑ Kayaking
☑ Beach volleyball

Facilities: Restaurant, bar and takeaway. Large shop (all season). Large aqua park, paddling pools, slides, jacuzzi. Games room. Multisports field, tennis, archery, minigolf, football. Theatre, evening entertainment, discos, show time spectacular. Riding. Bicycle hire. Off site: Resort of Argelès-sur-Mer and its beaches 2 km, as is karting, 10-pin bowling, amusement park and the site's private beach club Emeraude. Interesting old town of Collioure close by. Fishing 4 km. Golf 7 km.

Open: 17 April - 26 September.

Directions: Leave A9 motorway, exit 42, take D114, towards Argelès. Leave D114, exit 10 and follow signs for Plage Nord. Site is signed after first roundabout. Site on right 2 km. after last roundabout. GPS: 42.57093, 3.02906

Charges guide

Per unit incl. 1-3 persons and electricity	€ 26,00 - € 43,00
extra person	€ 6,00 - € 9,00
child (under 5 yrs)	€ 4,00 - € 6,00
dog	free

FRANCE – Peisey-Nancroix

Camping les Lanchettes

F-73210 Peisey-Nancroix (Savoie)
t: 04 79 07 93 07   e: lanchettes@free.fr
alanrogers.com/FR73030   www.camping-lanchettes.com

Accommodation: ☑Pitch ☑Mobile home/chalet ☐Hotel/B&B ☐Apartment

This site is in the beautiful Vanoise National Park and at 1,470 m. is one of the highest campsites in this guide. There is a steep climb to the site but the spectacular scenery is well worth the effort. It is a natural, terraced site with 90 good size, reasonably level and well drained, grassy/stony pitches, with 70 used for touring units, all having electricity (3-10A). Because of the altitude and cold winters there are no outside taps (warm bedding advised). For those who love walking and biking, the wonderful scenery, flora and fauna, this is the site for you. Under-powered units not advised. In winter it is ideal for the serious skier being close to the famous resort of Les Arcs (via free bus service and cable car) and about 30 of the pitches at the bottom of the site are unused as they become part of a cross country ski run. A wide range of footpaths and mountain bike rides is available in the valley and mountains around. Some chairlifts carry bikes up to the walking/bike tracks high up in the mountains; the descent is breathtaking.

Special offers
In summer, explore the mountains on a free conducted ramble. In winter, discover Paradiski, Peisey-Vallandry and Les Arcs on skis or explore the valley on snowshoes (racquettes).

You might like to know
In summer you can use the ski lifts to take your mountain bike up so as to experience the thrill of the descent as you would in winter on skis.

☑ Riding
☑ Pony trekking
☑ Mountain biking
☑ Golf
☑ Rafting
☑ Canyoning
☑ Rock climbing
☑ Aerial walkways
☑ Zip wires
☑ Fishing

☑ Rollerblading
☑ Paragliding
☑ Via Farrata
☑ Adventure park
☑ Skiing/winter sports

Facilities: Well appointed heated toilet block. Motorcaravan services. Restaurant, takeaway (July/Aug. and winter). Playground. Club/TV room. Large tent/marquee used in bad weather. In winter a small bus (free) runs to all the hotels, bars, ski tows. Off site: Walks in National Park. Riding next to site. Peisey-Nancroix, restaurants, bars and shops 3 km. Les Arcs winter sports centre 6 km. Outdoor swimming pool and bicycle hire 6 km. Golf and indoor pool 8 km. Lakeside beach 10 km.

Open: 15 December - 30 April and 1 June - 15 October.

Directions: From Albertville take N90 towards Bourg-St-Maurice, through Aime. In 9 km. turn right on D87, signed Peisey-Nancroix. Follow a winding hilly road (with hairpin bends) for 10 km. Pass through Peisey-Nancroix; the site is on the right about 1 km. beyond Nancroix. GPS: 45.53137, 6.77560

Charges guide

Per unit incl. 2 persons	€ 12,30 - € 13,80
extra person	€ 4,10 - € 4,60
child (2-7 yrs)	€ 2,30 - € 2,50
electricity (3-10A)	€ 3,10 - € 8,20

FRANCE – Le Grand-Bornand

Camping Caravaning l'Escale

Route de la Patinoire, F-74450 Le Grand-Bornand (Haute-Savoie)
t: **04 50 02 20 69** e: **contact@campinglescale.com**
alanrogers.com/FR74070 www.campinglescale.com

Accommodation: ☑Pitch ☑Mobile home/chalet ☐Hotel/B&B ☑Apartment

You are assured a good welcome in English from the Baur family at this beautifully maintained and picturesque site, situated at the foot of the Aravis mountain range. There are 149 pitches with 122 for touring. Of average size, part grass, part gravel they are separated by trees and shrubs that give a little shade. All pitches have electricity (2-10A) and 86 are fully serviced. Rock pegs are essential. A 200-year-old building houses a bar/restaurant decorated in traditional style and offering regional dishes in a delightful, warm ambience. The village is 200 m. away and has all the facilities of a resort with activities for summer and winter holidays. An excellent choice for an outdoor holiday, in summer a variety of well signed footpaths and cycle tracks provide forest or mountain excursions. In winter the area provides superb facilities for downhill and cross-country skiing. This very popular campsite, set beside the picture postcard ski resort of Le Grand-Bornand, has wonderful views.

Special offers
Special offers on rental accommodation (please see www.campinglescale.com). Short stays and one-night rentals are possible outside school holiday periods.

You might like to know
Campsite is open all year and rentals of mobile homes, apartments, studios and rooms are available throughout the year. A 240 m² pool (80 m² covered) with balnéo massaging jets is available in summer.

- ☑ Pony trekking
- ☑ Crafts
- ☑ Archery
- ☑ Golf
- ☑ Rock climbing
- ☑ Aerial walkways
- ☑ Zip wires
- ☑ Hot air ballooning
- ☑ Go-karting
- ☑ Fishing
- ☑ Indoor & outdoor pools
- ☑ Tennis
- ☑ Multisport court
- ☑ Skiing/winter sports
- ☑ Cycling *(road/off-road)*

Facilities: Good toilet blocks (heated in winter) have all the necessary facilities. Drying room for skis, clothing and boots. Superb pool complex with interconnected indoor (all season) and outdoor pools and paddling pools (15/6-29/8), jacuzzi and water jets. Cosy bar/restaurant and takeaway (all season). Play area. Tennis. WiFi. Activities for adults and children. Discounts on organised walks and visits to Chamonix-Mont Blanc. Off site: Village (5 minutes walk), shops, bars, restaurants, archery, paragliding, golf, minigolf. 150 km. of signed walks. Ice skating, snow shoes in winter. Bicycle hire 200 m. Riding and golf 3 km. Free bus for cable car (500 m) for skiing and snowboarding.

Open: 4 December - 18 April and 21 May - 26 September.

Directions: From Annecy follow D16 and D909 towards La Clusaz. At St Jean-de-Sixt, turn left at roundabout D4 signed Grand-Bornand. Just before village fork right signed Vallée de Bouchet and camping. Site entrance is on right at roundabout in 1.2 km. GPS: 45.94036, 6.42842

Charges guide

Per unit incl. 2 persons and electricity	€ 19,80 - € 29,40
extra person (over 2 yrs)	€ 4,90 - € 5,70
dog	€ 2,30

FRANCE – Saint Gervais-les-Bains

Camping les Dômes de Miage

197 route des Contamines, F-74170 Saint Gervais-les-Bains (Haute-Savoie)
t: 04 50 93 45 96 e: info@camping-mont-blanc.com
alanrogers.com/FR74140 www.camping-mont-blanc.com

Accommodation: ☑Pitch ☑Mobile home/chalet ☐ Hotel/B&B ☐ Apartment

Saint Gervais is a pretty spa town in the picturesque Val-Monjoie valley and this site
is 2 km. from its centre. It is 22 km. west of Chamonix and centrally located for
discovering this marvellous mountain region. Nestled among the mountains, this
sheltered, well equipped site provides 150 flat grassy pitches. Of a good size, about
half have shade and there are 100 with electricity points (3-10A). The remainder on
terraced ground are used for tents. Third generation hosts, Stéphane and Sophie, will
welcome you to the site and their passion for this area at the foot of Mont Blanc is
infectious. A number of Savoyard style chalets to let are planned for the future. This
is a good site for large motorcaravans. There is no on-site entertainment programme,
but a wealth of information about the area and activities available nearby is provided at
reception where they will help you plan your itinerary. The region is good for walking and
there is a bus service into Saint Gervais, from where there is a frequent shuttle bus to its
spa and a tramway to the Mont Blanc range.

You might like to know
Indoor and outdoor pools. Golf, fishing,
fitness/gym, rafting and canyoning, hiking
hot air ballooning, go-karting, summer sledge,
helicopter and plane flights at max. 25 km.

- ☑ Riding
- ☑ Pony trekking
- ☑ Tennis
- ☑ Archery
- ☑ Paintball
- ☑ Rock climbing
- ☑ Aerial walkways
- ☑ Zip wires
- ☑ Climbing wall
- ☑ 10-pin bowling

- ☑ Paragliding
- ☑ Via Ferrata
- ☑ Hydrospeed
- ☑ Canoeing/boating
- ☑ Cycling
  (road/off-road)

Facilities: Two sanitary blocks, one heated,
with a suite for disabled visitors and baby room.
Washing machines, dryer. Motorcaravan services.
Small basic shop. Bar/restaurant. TV room,
library, ironing board. Excellent playground.
Playing field. Off site: Fishing 100 m. Bicycle
hire 1 km. Riding 7 km. Shops, etc. and outdoor
swimming pool in St Gervais.

Open: 1 May - 12 September.

Directions: From St Gervais take the D902
towards Les Contamines and the site is on the
left after 2 km. GPS: 45.87389, 6.7199

Charges guide

Per unit incl. 2 persons and electricity	€ 19,40 - € 25,10
extra person	€ 3,00 - € 4,10
child (2-10 yrs)	€ 2,50 - € 3,50
dog	€ 2,00

FRANCE – Doussard

Campéole la Nublière

30 allée de la Nublière, F-74210 Doussard (Haute-Savoie)
t: 04 50 44 33 44 e: nubliere@wanadoo.fr
alanrogers.com/FR74190 www.campeole.com

Accommodation: ☑Pitch ☑Mobile home/chalet ☐ Hotel/B&B ☐ Apartment

If you are looking for large pitches, shady trees, mountain views and direct access to the lakeside beach, this site is for you. There are 271 touring pitches of which 243 have electrical hook-ups (6A). This area is very popular and the site is very likely to be busy in high season. There may be some noise from the road and the public beach. La Nublière is 16 km. from old Annecy and you are spoilt for choice in how to get there. Take a ferry trip, hire a sailing boat or pedalo, or walk or cycle along the traffic free track towards the town. The local beach and sailing club are close and there is a good restaurant on the site perimeter. Across the road from the site are courts for tennis and boules. The site is perfect for walking, cycling or sailing and in low season provides a tranquil base for those just wishing to relax in natural surroundings on the edge of a nature reserve.

You might like to know
Annecy old town is delightful and well worth a visit.

☑ Riding
☑ Tennis
☑ Golf
☑ Rafting
☑ Canyoning
☑ Canoeing
☑ Kayaking
☑ Hot air ballooning
☑ Fishing
☑ Paragliding

Facilities: Large clean sanitary blocks include free hot showers and good facilities for disabled people. Laundry. Shop (1/5-15/9). Restaurant on site perimeter (closed Mondays). Children's club (3/7-26/8) for 4-8 yrs. Safe deposit. Off site: Small supermarket adjacent to site. Good watersports area within 70 m. Access to town beach from site. Fishing 100 m. Golf and riding 4 km. Bicycle hire 7 km.

Open: 28 April - 18 September.

Directions: Site is 16 km. south of Annecy on Route d'Albertville, well signed. GPS: 45.7908, 6.2197

Charges guide

Per unit incl. 2 persons and electricity	€ 17,10 - € 26,60
extra person	€ 4,50 - € 6,80
child (2-6 yrs)	free - € 4,30

FRANCE – Excenevex
Campéole La Pinède

F-74140 Excenevex Plage (Haute-Savoie)
t: **04 50 72 85 05** e: nadine.ferran@atciat.com
alanrogers.com/FR74280 www.campeole.com

Accommodation: ☑Pitch ☑Mobile home/chalet ☐Hotel/B&B ☐Apartment

La Pinède is a member of the Campéole group and has direct access to Escenevex beach, the only naturally sandy beach on Lake Geneva. The site has a pleasant woodland setting and pitches are of a good size, mostly with electrical connections. Mobile homes, chalets and fully equipped tents are available for rent (including specially adapted units for wheelchair users). There is a supervised bathing area on the beach, which shelves gradually, and a small harbour (suitable only for boats with a shallow draught). Other amenities include a shop and takeaway food service, as well as an entertainment marquee and children's play area. There is plenty of activity here in high season with a children's club and regular discos and karaoke evenings. Geneva is just 25 km. distant and other possible excursions include Thonon-les-Bains with its weekly market and, of course, boat trips on Lake Geneva. Dramatic mountain scenery is close at hand, notably the spectacular Dent d'Oche and the Gorges du Pont du Diable.

You might like to know
Why not visit the lush botanical garden of Jaysinia in nearby Samoëns (free entry)?

☑ Riding
☑ Sailing
☑ Diving
☑ Rafting
☑ Canyoning
☑ Rock climbing
☑ Canoeing
☑ Fishing
☑ Hydrospeed
☑ Paragliding

Facilities: Lake beach. Takeaway food. Play area. Bouncy castle. Activities and entertainment programme. Tourist information. Mobile homes, chalets and equipped tents for rent. Off site: Geneva 25 km. Thonon-les-Bains 15 km. Hiking and cycle tracks. Riding. Golf

Open: 11 April - 11 September.

Directions: From Geneva head along the south side of the lake on the D1005 as far as Massongy and shortly beyond here take the northbound D324 to Escenevex. The site is well indicated from here. GPS: 46.34492, 6.35808

Charges guide

Per unit incl. 2 persons and electricity	€ 17,10 - € 26,60

FRANCE – Saint Aygulf

Camping Résidence du Campeur

B.P. 12, D7, F-83371 Saint Aygulf (Var)
t: 04 94 81 01 59 e: info@residence-campeur.com
alanrogers.com/FR83050 www.residence-campeur.com

Accommodation: ☑Pitch ☑Mobile home/chalet ☐ Hotel/B&B ☐ Apartment

This excellent site near the Côte d'Azur will take you away from all the bustle of the Mediterranean coast. Spread out over ten hectares, there are separate areas for mobile homes and touring caravans and tents, with pitches arranged along avenues. The 67 touring pitches average 100 m² in size and all have electricity connections and private sanitary facilities (although washbasins double as dishwashing sinks). The bar/restaurant is surrounded by a shady terrace, whilst friendly staff provide an excellent service. A pleasant pool complex is available for those who wish to stay on site instead of going swimming in the nearby lake or from the Mediterranean beaches. Activities are organised daily during the summer season and the site has its own open air cinema.

You might like to know
This region is perhaps best known for its fine sandy beaches and one of the best is just 2.5 km. from this site.

☑ Riding
☑ Tennis
☑ Cycling (road)
☑ Sports field
☑ Outdoor pool
☑ Archery
☑ Golf
☑ Fishing
☑ Petanque
☑ Minigolf

Facilities: Private toilet blocks are cleaned at regular intervals and include a washbasin, shower and WC. Laundry area with washing machines. Well stocked supermarket. Bar/restaurant. Takeaway (all open all season). New swimming pool complex with four water slides (high season). Two tennis courts. Minigolf. Boules. Fishing. Bicycle hire. Play area. Games/TV room. Only gas or electric barbecues are permitted. Off site: Riding 1.5 km. Golf 2 km. Beach and St Aygulf 2.5 km. Water skiing nearby.

Open: 27 March - 30 September.

Directions: Leave A8 at Le Muy exit (no. 36) on N555 towards Draguignan then onto the N7 towards Fréjus. Turn right on D7 signed St Aygulf and site is on the right about 2.5 km. before the town. GPS: 43.40905, 6.70893

Charges guide

Per unit incl. 3 persons and electricity	€ 30,10 - € 50,15
extra person	€ 5,19 - € 8,65
child (under 7 yrs)	€ 3,54 - € 5,90
dog	€ 4,00

Camping Resort la Baume – la Palmeraie

3775 rue des Combattants d'Afrique du Nord, F-83618 Fréjus (Var)
t: 04 94 19 88 88   e: reception@labaume-lapalmeraie.com
alanrogers.com/FR83060   www.labaume-lapalmeraie.com

Accommodation: ☑Pitch ☑Mobile home/chalet ☐ Hotel/B&B ☐ Apartment

La Baume is a large, busy site about 5.5 km. from the long sandy beach of Fréjus-Plage, although with its fine and varied selection of swimming pools, many people do not bother to make the trip. The pools with their palm trees are remarkable for their size and variety (water slides, etc) – the very large 'feature' pool a highlight. There is an aquatic play area and two indoor pools with a slide and a spa area. The site has nearly 250 adequately sized, fully serviced pitches, with some separators and most have shade. Although tents are accepted, the site concentrates mainly on caravanning. It becomes full in season. Adjoining La Baume is its sister site La Palmeraie, providing self-catering accommodation, its own landscaped pool and offering some entertainment to supplement that at La Baume. There are 500 large pitches with mains sewerage for mobile homes. La Baume's convenient location has its downside as there is some traffic noise on a few pitches from the nearby autoroute – somewhat obtrusive at first but we soon failed to notice it.

Special offers
Free admission to the large 'Base Nature' in Fréjus with a wide range of sporting activities and facilities including cyclo-cross, mountain biking, rollerblading ramps, skateboarding and BMX.

You might like to know
Mountain bike hire from April to September. Municipal shuttle-buses to the beach and watersports centre.

☑ Riding
☑ Pony trekking
☑ Tennis
☑ Archery
☑ Diving
☑ Golf
☑ Aerial walkways
☑ Zip wires
☑ Canoeing
☑ Kayaking

☑ Fitness/gym
☑ Fishing
☑ Go-karting & quad bikes
☑ Indoor & outdoor pools

Facilities: Seven refurbished toilet blocks. Supermarket, several shops. Two bars, terrace overlooking pools, TV. Restaurant, takeaway. Six swimming pools (heated all season, two covered, plus steam room and jacuzzi). Fitness centre. Tennis. Archery (July/Aug). Skateboard park. Organised events, daytime and evening entertainment, some English. Amphitheatre. Discos all season. Children's club (all season). Two play areas renewed. Off site: Bus to Fréjus passes gate. Riding 2 km. Fishing 3 km. Golf 5 km. Beach 5 km.

Open: 27 March - 25 September (with full services).

Directions: From west, A8, exit Fréjus, take the N7 southwest (Fréjus). After 4 km, turn left on the D4 and site is 3 km. From east, A8, exit 38 Fréjus and follow signs for Cais. Site is signed. GPS: 43.45998, 6.72048

Charges guide

Per unit incl. 2 persons, electricity, water and drain	€ 19,00 - € 45,00
extra person	€ 5,00 - € 13,00
child (under 7 yrs)	free - € 7,00
dog	€ 4,00 - € 5,00

Min. stay for motorhomes 2 nights.
Large units should book.

FRANCE – Roquebrune-sur-Argens

Kawan Village les Pêcheurs

F-83520 Roquebrune-sur-Argens (Var)
t: 04 94 45 71 25 e: info@camping-les-pecheurs.com
alanrogers.com/FR83200 www.camping-les-pecheurs.com

Accommodation: ☑Pitch ☑Mobile home/chalet ☐Hotel/B&B ☐Apartment

Les Pêcheurs will appeal to families who appreciate natural surroundings together with many activities, cultural and sporting. Interspersed with mobile homes, the 150 good sized touring pitches (6/10A electricity) are separated by trees or flowering bushes. The Provencal style buildings are delightful, especially the bar, restaurant and games room, with its terrace down to the river and the site's own canoe station (locked gate). Across the road is a lake used exclusively for water skiing with a sandy beach, a restaurant and minigolf. Enlarged spa facilities include swimming pool, large jacuzzi, massage, steam pool and a sauna. Developed over three generations by the Simoncini family, this peaceful, friendly site is set in more than four hectares of mature, well shaded countryside at the foot of the Roquebrune Rock. Activities include climbing the 'Rock' with a guide. We became more and more intrigued with stories about the Rock and the Holy Hole, the Three Crosses and the Hermit all call for further exploration. The medieval village of Roquebrune is within walking distance.

You might like to know

There is a diving school on site – an ideal environment to learn to dive.

- ☑ Riding
- ☑ Cycling (road)
- ☑ Sports field
- ☑ Outdoor pool
- ☑ Diving
- ☑ Waterskiing
- ☑ Golf
- ☑ Rafting
- ☑ Canoeing
- ☑ Fishing

Facilities: Modern, refurbished, well designed toilet blocks, baby baths, facilities for disabled visitors. Washing machines. Shop. Bar and restaurant (all open all season). Heated outdoor swimming pool (all season), separate paddling pool (lifeguard in high season), ice cream bar. Games room. Spa facilities. Playing field. Fishing. Canoeing. Waterskiing. Rafting and diving schools. Activities for children and adults (high season), visits to local wine caves. Only gas or electric barbecues. WiFi in reception, bar and pool area. Off site: Bicycle hire 1 km. Riding 5 km. Golf 5 km. (reduced fees).

Open: 1 April - 30 September.

Directions: From A8 take Le Muy exit, follow the N7 towards Fréjus for 13 km. bypassing Le Muy. After crossing A8, turn right at roundabout towards Roquebrune-sur-Argens. Site is on left after 1 km. just before bridge over river. GPS: 43.450783, 6.6335

Charges guide

Per unit incl. 2 persons and electricity	€ 23,00 - € 43,00
extra person	€ 4,00 - € 7,80
child (5-10 yrs)	€ 3,20 - € 6,20
dog (max. 1)	€ 3,20

FRANCE – Fréjus

Camping Holiday Green

Route de Bagnols, F-83600 Fréjus (Var)
t: 04 94 19 88 30 e: info@holidaygreen.com
alanrogers.com/FR83600 www.holidaygreen.com

Accommodation: ☑Pitch ☑Mobile home/chalet ☐ Hotel/B&B ☐ Apartment

Holiday Green is seven kilometres inland from Fréjus. It is a large, modern campsite with a fantastic view of the red massif of Esterel – very impressive as you arrive. The site has been developed on a hillside, by reception at the top of the hill is a large Californian style outside swimming pool as well as a new covered and heated swimming pool and waterslide. The rest of the site is terraced into the hillside and almost completely hidden in the 15 hectares of pine woods which absorbs about 500 mobile homes and some 54 touring pitches. Sloping in parts, there is plenty of shade and electricity (6/13A) available. The pool complex on the site is the centre of all the fun and it is said there are activities and entertainment from morning until closing. The site provides a free daily bus (1/7-31/8) for the beach and Aquatica, the biggest aquapark in the region, with Europe's largest wave pool (open 7/6-14/9).

Special offers
Organised mountain bike trips. Special rates on sub aqua courses in the site pool.

You might like to know
Aquagym every day from 1 April to 30 September.

☑ Riding
☑ Tennis
☑ Cycling *(road)*
☑ Mountain biking
☑ Outdoor pool
☑ Archery
☑ Sailing
☑ Diving
☑ Fitness/gym

Facilities: Modern toilet facilities include good hot showers. Laundry. Shopping centre. Bar, restaurant, fast food. Soundproofed disco. Swimming pool. Three tennis courts. Archery. Petanque. All open all season. Excursions on foot, on horseback and on mountain bikes (to hire) offering the chance to explore the countryside. Entertainment programme of dances, concerts and festivals. Playground. Children's club (July/Aug). No charcoal barbecues. Off site: Bus route outside entrance. Beach 8 km. Golf 8 km.

Open: 1 April - 30 September.

Directions: From A8 autoroute exit 38 follow signs for Bagnols-en-Forêt about 2 km. back over the autoroute, and the site is clearly signed at roundabout. GPS: 43.48563, 6.71745

Charges guide

Per unit incl. 2 persons and electricity	€ 27,00 - € 47,00

72

FRANCE – Saint Julien-des-Landes

Castel Camping la Garangeoire

F-85150 Saint Julien-des-Landes (Vendée)
t: **02 51 46 65 39** e: **info@garangeoire.com**
alanrogers.com/FR85040 www.camping-la-garangeoire.com

Accommodation: ☑Pitch ☑Mobile home/chalet ☐Hotel/B&B ☐Apartment

La Garangeoire is a stunning campsite, situated some 15 km. inland, near the village of St Julien-des-Landes. Set in 200 ha. of parkland surrounding the small château of La Garangeoire of which there is an outstanding view as you approach through the gates. With a spacious, relaxed atmosphere, the main camping areas are on either side of the old road which is edged with mature trees. The 360 pitches, all named after birds, are individually hedged, some with shade. They are well spaced and are especially large (most 150-200 m²), most with electricity (8A) and some with water and drainage also. Access is good for large units. Tour operators use 144 pitches. The parkland provides peaceful fields and woods for walking and three lakes, one of which is used for fishing and boating (life jackets are provided). The site is now run by the third generation of owners since 1964, Ann and Eric Bourgon.

Special offers
On site: four signposted trails, riding centre with two qualified instructors, three fishing lakes, football pitch with soccer school in high season and pedal-karting circuit.

You might like to know
Sailing and surfing in Brétignolles sur Mer (12 km). Golf course in Coëx (8 km). Nature trails around the Lac de Jaunay (2 km).

☑ Riding
☑ Pony trekking
☑ Tennis
☑ Mountain biking
☑ Outdoor pool
☑ Archery
☑ Canoeing
☑ Pedaloes
☑ Go-karting
☑ Fishing

☑ Covered pool
☑ Paintball *(2 km)*
☑ Zip wire *(2 km)*
☑ Aerial walkways *(2 km)*
☑ Golf *(8 km)*

Facilities: Ample, first class sanitary facilities. All have washbasins in cabins. Facilities for babies and disabled people. Laundry facilities. Motorcaravan service point. Shop, full restaurant and takeaway (10/5-22/9) with bars and terrace (all season). Pool complex with water slides, fountains and a children's pool (all season). Play field with play equipment. Games room. Two tennis courts. Bicycle hire. Minigolf. Archery. Riding (July/Aug). Fishing and boating. Bouncy castle. Six Trampolines. Quadricycles (on payment).
Off site: Golf 10 km. Beaches 15 km.

Open: 24 April - 25 September.

Directions: Site is signed from St Julien; entrance is to the east off the D21 road, 2.5 km. north of St Julien-des-Landes.
GPS: 46.66387, -1.71346

Charges guide

Per unit incl. 2 persons and electricity	€ 17,50 - € 36,50
incl. services	€ 19,50 - € 39,00
extra person	€ 4,50 - € 7,80
child (under 10 yrs)	€ 2,50 - € 3,60
dog	€ 3,00 - € 3,50

FRANCE – Saint Julien-des-Landes

Camping Domaine de la Forêt

Route de Martinet, F-85150 Saint Julien-des-Landes (Vendée)
t: 02 51 46 62 11 e: camping@domainelaforet.com
alanrogers.com/FR85820 www.domainelaforet.com

Accommodation: ☑Pitch ☑Mobile home/chalet ☐ Hotel/B&B ☐ Apartment

Set in the tranquil and beautiful natural parkland surrounding an 18th century château, this lovely site has 200 large pitches, of which 167 are for touring units. All are on grass and fully serviced, including 6A electricity, some are in shady woodland and others for sun-worshippers are more open. The camping area is only a small part of the 50 hectare estate, with a mix of woodland, open meadows and fishing lakes, all accessible to campers. The many outbuildings around the courtyard have been tastefully converted and include a bar and restaurant in the old stables. There are two outdoor swimming pools, one on each side of the château. Many sports, activities and entertainment are on offer which should keep everyone satisfied. Children will have a great time here, exploring the vast, unrestricted area and sometimes hidden corners of this site in 'Swallows and Amazons' style. However, parents should note there are open, unfenced fishing lakes and barns with tractors and machinery. The attractive small village with shops and services is within walking distance.

You might like to know
Why not visit Le Puy du Fou? The evening spectacle is world-class and highly recommended. During the day the Grand Parc with its wildlife park, its floral park and entertainment is also a trip well worth making.

- ☑ Riding
- ☑ Tennis
- ☑ Sports field
- ☑ Outdoor pool
- ☑ Sailing
- ☑ Golf
- ☑ Canoeing
- ☑ Go-karting
- ☑ Fishing
- ☑ Quad bikes

Facilities: Two large good quality sanitary blocks include washbasins in cubicles, with good provision for babies and disabled campers. Laundry facilities with washing machines and dryers. Bar/restaurant with TV. Two heated outdoor swimming pools (one for children with slide, one for serious swimmers). Regular evening entertainment, children's clubs and disco (July/Aug). Adventure playground, trampoline and games room. Tennis. Boules. Fishing lakes. 6 hole swing-golf course (pitch and putt with soft balls) and minigolf. Canoeing trips. WiFi. Only gas barbecues permitted. No double axle caravans accepted. Off site: Equestrian centre, bicycle hire 200 m. Golf and beaches 12 km.

Open: 15 May - 15 September.

Directions: St Julien-des-Landes is 25 km. west of La Roche-sur-Yon, northwest of La Mothe-Achard. From La Mothe-Achard take D12 to St Julien, turn northeast on D55 at crossroads towards Martinet. Site is on left almost immediately (signed). GPS: 46.6432, -1.71198

Charges guide

Per unit incl. 2 persons	€ 14,50 - € 29,00
extra person	€ 3,00 - € 6,00
child (under 10 yrs)	€ 3,00 - € 4,50
electricity (6A)	€ 3,00 - € 4,00

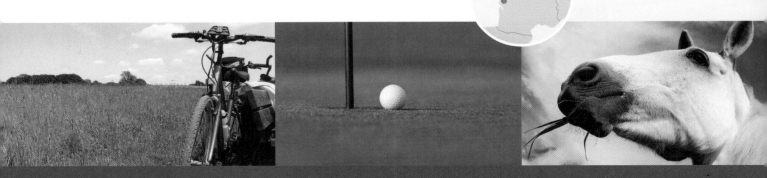

Kawan Village Lac de Bouzey

19 rue du Lac, F-88390 Sanchey (Vosges)
t: **03 29 82 49 41** e: **lacdebouzey@orange.fr**
alanrogers.com/FR88040 www.lacdebouzey.com

Accommodation: ☑Pitch ☑Mobile home/chalet ☐Hotel/B&B ☐Apartment

Open all year, Camping Lac de Bouzey is 8 km. west of Épinal, at the start of the Vosges Massif. The 160 reasonably level grass pitches are separated by very tall trees and some hedging giving varying amounts of shade. There are 121 for touring, all with electricity (6-10A) and 100 fully serviced. They are on a gently sloping hillside above the lake and have views over the lake and its sandy beaches. In high season there is entertainment for all ages, especially teenagers and in high season the site will be very lively. English is spoken. Many watersports may be enjoyed, from pedaloes to canoes, windsurfing and sailing. The large, imposing building at the entrance to the site houses a restaurant and bar with terraces overlooking the lake and the underground disco. Two bars by the lake would indicate that the lakeside is popular with the public in summer but the camping area is quiet, separated by a road and well back and above the main entrance. It is well placed for exploring the hills, valleys, lakes and waterfalls of the south of Alsace Lorraine.

Special offers

The entertainment team organise nightly shows and a Kids Club. Accompanied walks are arranged in the surrounding forest to discover the local flora and fauna.

You might like to know

Bicycle hire available. Many superb drives in the area including la Route des Crêtes la Route des Vins (with dégustation!) and la Vallée des Lacs. Local maps available at reception.

☑ Riding
☑ Pony trekking
☑ Archery
☑ Sailing
☑ Paintball
☑ Rock climbing
☑ Aerial walkways
☑ Go-karting
☑ 10-pin bowling
☑ Fishing

☑ Tennis
☑ Short tennis
☑ Canoeing & pedaloes
☑ Cycling *(road/off-road)*
☑ Rafting & canyoning

Facilities: The refurbished toilet block includes a baby room and one for disabled people (there is up and down hill walking). Small, heated section in the main building with toilet, washbasin and shower is used in winter. Laundry facilities. Motorcaravan service point. Shop, bar, restaurant and takeaway (all season). Heated pool (1/5-30/9). Fishing. Riding. Games room. Archery. Bicycle hire. Internet access. Soundproofed room for cinema shows and discos (high season). Lake beach, bathing and boating. Off site: Golf 8 km.

Open: All year.

Directions: Site is 8 km. west of Épinal on the D460. From Épinal follow signs for Lac de Bouzey and Sanchey. At western end of Sanchey turn south, site signed.
GPS: 48.16692, 6.35990

Charges guide

Per unit incl. 2 persons and electricity	€ 23,00 - € 34,00
extra person	€ 6,00 - € 10,00
child (4-10 yrs)	free - € 7,00
dog	free - € 4,00

Stowford Farm Meadows

Berry Down, Combe Martin, Ilfracombe EX34 0PW (Devon)
t: **01271 882476** e: **enquiries@stowford.co.uk**
alanrogers.com/UK0690 **www.stowford.co.uk**

Accommodation: ☑Pitch ☑Mobile home/chalet ☐Hotel/B&B ☐Apartment

Stowford Farm is a friendly, family park set in 500 acres of the rolling North Devon countryside, available for recreation and walking, yet within easy reach of five local beaches. The touring park and its facilities have been developed in the fields and farm buildings surrounding the attractive old farmhouse and provide a village like centre with a comfortable spacious feel. There are 710 pitches on five slightly sloping meadows separated by Devon hedges of beech and ash. The numbered and marked pitches, some with hardstanding, are accessed by hard roads, most have electricity (10/16A) and there are well placed water points. There is much for children to do, from the indoor heated pool and under cover mini-zoo (Petorama), where they can handle many sorts of animals (on payment), to the wide range of organised activities on offer. In low season some facilities may only open for limited hours. Stowford also provides plenty to keep the whole family occupied without leaving the park, including woodland walks and horse riding from the park's own stables.

You might like to know
There are 500 acres of rolling Devon countryside, mature woodland and lush green caravan and camping meadows lined with beech and ash trees.

- ☑ Riding
- ☑ Pony trekking
- ☑ Cycling *(road)*
- ☑ Sports field
- ☑ Sailing
- ☑ Golf
- ☑ Hiking
- ☑ Fishing
- ☑ Woodland walks

Facilities: Five identical toilet blocks, each looked after by resident wardens, are fully equipped and provide good, functional facilities, each block with laundry facilities and dishwashing. The newest block (in field 5) has under-floor heating and includes facilities for disabled visitors. Extra good facilities for disabled visitors and private family washrooms are beside reception. Well stocked shop. Takeaway with restaurant area. Bars and entertainment in season. Indoor pool (22x10 m; heated Easter-Oct) at a small charge. Riding. 18-hole pitch and putt. Crazy golf. 'Large play area. Games and activities organised in high season. WiFi. ATM. Woodland walks. Max. 2 dogs. Off site: Fishing and boat launching 4 miles. Bicycle hire 10 miles.

Open: All year.

Directions: From Barnstaple take A39 towards Lynton. After 1 mile turn left on B3230. Turn right at garage on A3123 and park is 1.5 miles on the right. GPS: 51.174983, -4.05475

Charges guide

Per unit incl. 2 persons and electricity	£ 9,40 - £ 28,00
extra person	free - £ 4,50

Low and mid season discounts for over 50s.

Woodlands Caravan Park

Holt Road, Upper Sheringham NR26 8TU (Norfolk)
t: **01263 823802** e: **enquiries@woodlandscaravanpark.co.uk**
alanrogers.com/UK3435 **www.woodlandscaravanpark.co.uk**

Accommodation: ☑Pitch ☑Mobile home/chalet ☐Hotel/B&B ☐Apartment

This pleasantly wooded caravan park is set in the beautiful surroundings of North Norfolk's protected heathland, next to Sheringham Park (National Trust). There are many lovely walks all around the area, including one to the beach (1.5 miles). The park is within easy reach of Holt, Cromer and Sheringham, with the major bird watching areas of Blakeney, Cley and Salthouse also within 30 minutes drive. There are 225 touring pitches in two main areas for caravans and motorcaravans (tents are not accepted). Electricity (10A) is available to most. The excellent Pinewood Park Leisure Club is adjacent to the park offering swimming and other fitness facilities at a discounted rate for those staying at Woodlands.

You might like to know
Guests at Woodlands are entitled to discounted rates at the adjacent Pinewood Park Leisure Complex. There you will find a 25 m. heated indoor pool and children's pool, fitness studio with cardio/resistance machines and free weights, swedish sauna, steam room and spa bath.

☑ Riding
☑ Cycling
☑ Crafts
☑ Sailing
☑ Golf
☑ Hiking
☑ Fishing
☑ Sauna
☑ Gym

Facilities: Three well maintained toilet blocks provide good facilities and include facilities for disabled visitors, baby changing and laundry. Well stocked shop. Gas supplies. Lounge bar and family bar with musical entertainment most weekends. Barbecues. Play area (2 acres, fenced and gated). Pinewood Park Leisure Club with indoor pool, gym, sauna. etc (all year). Off site: Golf and bicycle hire 1.5 miles. Fishing and riding 3 miles.

Open: March - October.

Directions: From Cromer on the A148 towards Holt, pass signs for Sheringham Park and site is on right just before Bodham village. From Holt on A148 just after Bodham, site is on left, well signed. GPS: 52.92363, 1.19444

Charges guide

Per unit incl. electricity	£ 15,50 - £ 18,50
awning	£ 2,50

Rivendale Caravan & Leisure Park

Buxton Road, Alsop-en-le-Dale, Ashbourne DE6 1QU (Derbyshire)
t: **01335 310311** e: **enquiries@rivendalecaravanpark.co.uk**
alanrogers.com/UK3850 www.rivendalecaravanpark.co.uk

Accommodation: ☑Pitch ☑Mobile home/chalet ☑Hotel/B&B ☐ Apartment

This unusual park has been developed in the bowl of a hill quarry which was last worked over 50 years ago. The steep quarry walls shelter three sides with marvellous views over the Peak National Park countryside to the south. A wide access road passes the renovated stone building which houses reception, a shop, bar and a café/restaurant. It gently climbs to a horseshoe shaped area providing 136 pitches some of which are rather small but most are of a generous size, with 16A electricity. The pitches are a mixture of hardstanding and grass, and are divided by shrubs. A further, open, marked grass area is accessed by hardcore roads. The park takes up about 11 acres and a further 26 acres belong to the owners with certain parts suitable for walking – a must to appreciate the Derbyshire countryside with its dry stone walls, wild flowers and a little more of the quarry history. The park is situated almost on the Tissington Trail for walking or off road cycling and linking with the High Peak and Monsal Dale Trail. Other spectacular walks and cycle rides run along the Manifold, Wye and Dove valleys.

Special offers
Free walking map with more than 2 nights booked in pods, yurts, lodges or B&B.

You might like to know
The local River Dove was the famous trout stream in Izaak Walton's book 'The Complete Angler'.

- ☑ Pony trekking
- ☑ Mountain biking
- ☑ Sailing
- ☑ Golf
- ☑ Rock climbing
- ☑ Hiking
- ☑ Canoeing
- ☑ Climbing wall
- ☑ Fishing
- ☑ Bird watching

- ☑ Off-roading 4WD
- ☑ Hot air ballooning

Facilities: First rate toilet facilities include some washbasins in cubicles for ladies, and an excellent en-suite room for disabled visitors. Laundry room. Shop (all essentials). Bar (evenings) and café with home-made and local food (open mornings, lunch and evenings, both with limited opening in low season). Packed lunches from reception. Special events monthly and games in main season. Hot tubs for hire, delivered to your pitch. WiFi. For rent on the park are 4 B&B rooms, a luxury caravan holiday home and a yurt (6 persons). Off site: Bicycle hire and riding 5 miles. Sailing and boat launching 8 miles. Fishing and golf 10 miles.

Open: All year excl. 9 January - 2 February.

Directions: Park is 7 miles north of Ashbourne on the A515 to Buxton, on the eastern side of the road. It is well signed between the turnings east to Alsop Moor and Matlock (A5012), but take care as this is a very fast section of the A515. GPS: 53.106383, -1.760567

Charges guide

Per unit incl. 2 persons and electricity	£ 14,50 - £ 19,00
extra person	£ 2,50
child (4-15 yrs)	£ 2,00
dog	£ 1,00

Croft Farm Water & Leisure Park

Bredon's Hardwick, Tewkesbury GL20 7EE (Gloucestershire)
t: **01684 772321**   e: **enquiries@croftfarmleisure.co.uk**
alanrogers.com/UK4150   www.croftfarmleisure.co.uk

Accommodation: ☑Pitch ☑Mobile home/chalet ☐ Hotel/B&B ☐ Apartment

Croft Farm is an AALA licensed Watersports Centre with Royal Yachting Association approved tuition available for windsurfing, sailing, kayaking and canoeing. The lakeside campsite has around 96 level pitches, with electric hook-ups (10A), but there are many seasonal units, leaving around 36 pitches for tourists, plus some tent pitches. There are 36 gravel hardstandings with very little shade or shelter. 'Gym and Tonic' is a fully equipped gymnasium with qualified instructors, sunbed and sauna. Sports massage, aromatherapy and beauty treatments are available by appointment. Activity holidays for families and groups are organised. Campers can use their own non-powered boats on the lake with reduced launching fees and there is river fishing. There are plans to include a launch ramp onto the river. Climb Bredon Hill (2 miles) for a panoramic view of the Severn and Avon Valleys. Places of interest include Bredon Barn, pottery and church, and the historic town of Tewkesbury with its Abbey, theatre and indoor swimming pool.

Special offers
Accommodation can be provided in camping pods and catering is available from the lakeside café and bar.

You might like to know
The watersports school has wide experience in providing tuition for individuals families and groups on the lake and nearby River Avon. Sailing boats windsurfers and canoes are available to hire.

☑ Riding
☑ Archery
☑ Sailing
☑ Windsurfing
☑ Rafting
☑ Canoeing
☑ Kayaking
☑ Pedaloes
☑ Fitness/gym
☑ Fishing

Facilities: A recently modernised building has excellent facilities with spacious hot showers. A heated unit in the main building is always open and best for cooler months; this provides further WCs, washbasins and showers, laundry and facilities for disabled persons. Gas. Cafe/bar (Fri-Sun low season, daily at other times). Takeaway. Gym. Playground. River fishing. Barrier and toilet block key (£5 deposit). Fenced dog exercise area. WiFi in the clubhouse. Off site: Pub opposite. Tewkesbury 1.5 miles. Golf 3 miles. Riding 8 miles.

Open: 1 March - 31 December.

Directions: Bredon's Hardwick is midway between Tewkesbury and Bredon on B4080. Site entrance opposite 'Cross Keys Inn'. From M5 exit 9 take A438 (Tewkesbury), at first lights turn right into Shannon Way. Turn right into Northway Lane, cross motorway bridge. Turn left into housing estate. At T-junction turn right on B4080, site is on left. GPS: 52.015967, -2.130267

Charges guide

Per unit incl. 2 persons, electricity and awning	£ 16,00
extra person (over 3 yrs)	£ 3,50
dog	£ 1,00

Weekends min. 2 nights stay. B.Hs min. 3 nights.

Tummel Valley Holiday Park

Tummel Bridge, Pitlochry PH16 5SA (Perth and Kinross)
t: **01882 634221** e: **enquiries@parkdeanholidays.co.uk**
alanrogers.com/UK7305 www.parkdeanholidays.co.uk

Accommodation: ☑Pitch ☑Mobile home/chalet ☐Hotel/B&B ☐Apartment

Set in the Tay Forest Park on the banks of the River Tummel, this large family holiday park is part of the Parkdean Group. Divided into two areas by the roadway, the main emphasis is on chalets to let on the side that overlooks the river. Privately owned caravan holiday homes and touring pitches are on the other, quieter side. The 26 touring pitches, open plan with hardstanding, electricity hook-up and a shared water point, overlook a small fishing lake which is an added attraction for all the family. On arrival, you should turn right and park, then cross back to book in. The leisure complex with indoor and outdoor activities is on the river side, as is the reception office.

You might like to know

A regular bus service leaves from close to the site entrance with the opportunity to explore the Perthshire Highlands.

- ☑ Riding
- ☑ Cycling (road)
- ☑ Sports field
- ☑ Outdoor pool
- ☑ Golf
- ☑ Fishing
- ☑ Nature trails
- ☑ Sauna
- ☑ Adventure play area

Facilities: The very clean toilet block has vanity style washbasins, pre-set showers and a bathroom in each section. Good facilities for disabled visitors. Well equipped laundry. Chemical disposal but no motorcaravan service point. Shop. Riverside entertainment complex with bar and terrace, restaurant and takeaway. Indoor heated pool and toddlers' splash pool. Solarium and sauna. Amusements. Separate area with pool tables. All weather sports court. Adventure play area. Crazy golf. Nature trails. Bicycle hire. Fishing. Note: all venues are non-smoking. Max. 2 dogs per unit. Off site: Golf and riding 10 miles. Buses leave near park entrance.

Open: 24 March - 1 November.

Directions: Travel through Pitlochry. After 2 miles turn left on B8019 to Tummel Bridge (10 miles). Park is on both the left and right. Tourers should turn right and park, then return to reception on the left. GPS: 56.70742, -4.02002

Charges guide

Per unit incl. 4 persons and electricity	£ 13,00 - £ 32,00
dog	£ 2,00 - £ 3,00

Forest Holidays Glenmore

Aviemore PH22 1QU (Highland)
t: **01479 861271**   e: **info@forestholidays.co.uk**
alanrogers.com/UK7680   www.forestholidays.co.uk

Accommodation: ☑Pitch ☑Mobile home/chalet ☐Hotel/B&B ☐Apartment

Forest Holidays is a partnership between the Forestry Commission and the Camping and Caravanning Club. This site is attractively laid out in a fairly informal style in several adjoining areas connected by narrow, part gravel, part tarmac roads, with access to the lochside. One of these areas, the Pinewood Area, is very popular and has 32 hardstandings (some distance from the toilet block). Of the 260 marked pitches on fairly level, firm grass, 122 have electricity (16A). This site with something for everyone would be great for family holidays. The Glenmore Forest Park lies close to the sandy shore of Loch Morlich amidst conifer woods and surrounded on three sides by the impressive Cairngorm mountains. It is conveniently situated for a range of activities, including skiing (extensive lift system), orienteering, hill and mountain walking (way-marked walks), fishing (trout and pike) and non-motorized watersports on the Loch.

You might like to know
Why not join in one of the Forest Survival weekends? These aim to equip you with some of the skills you would need to survive alone in the forest. Great fun for all the family!

☑ Mountain biking
☑ Archery
☑ Golf
☑ Rock climbing
☑ Skiing *(downhill)*
☑ Canoeing
☑ Fishing
☑ Orienteering
☑ Den building
☑ Abseiling

Facilities: New toilet and shower blocks. Next to the site is a range of amenities including a well stocked shop (open all year), a café serving a variety of meals and snacks, and a Forestry Commission visitor centre and souvenir shop. Barbecues are not permitted in dry weather. Sandy beach. Off site: The Aviemore centre with a wide range of indoor and outdoor recreation activities including skiing 7 miles. Golf within 15 miles. Fishing and boat trips.

Open: All year.

Directions: Immediately south of Aviemore on B9152 (not A9 bypass) take B970 then follow sign for Cairngorm and Loch Morlich. Site entrance is on right past the loch.
GPS: 57.167033, -3.694717

Charges guide

Per unit incl. 2 persons	£ 11,00 - £ 25,50
extra person	£ 5,25 - £ 8,25
child	£ 2,75 - £ 4,25

Discounts for families, disabled guests and senior citizens.

Glen Nevis Caravan Park

Glen Nevis, Fort William PH33 6SX (Highland)
t: **01397 702191** e: **camping@glen-nevis.co.uk**
alanrogers.com/UK7830 www.glen-nevis.co.uk

Accommodation: ☑Pitch ☑Mobile home/chalet ☐Hotel/B&B ☐Apartment

Just outside Fort William, in a most attractive and quiet situation with views of Ben Nevis, this spacious park is used by those on active pursuits as well as sightseeing tourists. It comprises eight quite spacious fields, divided between caravans, motorcaravans and tents (steel pegs required). It is licensed for 250 touring caravans but with no specific tent limits. The large touring pitches, many with hardstanding, are marked with wooden fence dividers, 174 with electricity and 100 also have water and drainage. The park becomes full in the peak months but there are vacancies each day. If reception is closed (possible in low season) you site yourself. The park's own modern restaurant and bar with good value bar meals is a short stroll from the park, open to all. A well managed park with a bustling, but pleasing ambience, watched over by Ben Nevis, around 1,000 acres of the Glen Nevis estate are open to campers to see the wildlife and explore this lovely area.

You might like to know
Fort William is the outdoor capital of the UK, home to Britain's highest mountain and some of the finest scenery that Europe has to offer.

- ☑ Mountain biking
- ☑ Diving
- ☑ Golf
- ☑ Canyoning
- ☑ Rock climbing
- ☑ Hiking
- ☑ Kayaking
- ☑ 10-pin bowling
- ☑ Fishing
- ☑ Sailing
- ☑ Skiing
- ☑ Snowboarding
- ☑ Ice climbing

Facilities: The four modern toilet blocks with showers (extra showers in two blocks); and units for visitors with disabilities. An excellent block in Nevis Park (one of the eight camping fields) has some washbasins in cubicles, showers, further facilities for disabled visitors, a second large laundry room and dishwashing sinks. Motorcaravan service point. Shop (Easter-mid Oct), barbecue area and snack bar (May-mid Sept). Play area on bark. Off site: Pony trekking, golf and fishing near.

Open: 15 March - 31 October.

Directions: Turn off A82 to east at roundabout just north of Fort William following camp sign. GPS: 56.804517, -5.073917

Charges guide

Per person	£ 1,60 - £ 2,50
child (5-15 yrs)	£ 0,80 - £ 1,30
pitch incl. awning	£ 4,40 - £ 12,00
serviced pitch plus	£ 2,00 - £ 3,00

IRELAND – Tipperary

Ballinacourty House Caravan Park

Glen of Aherlow, Tipperary (Co. Tipperary)
t: 062 565 59   e: info@camping.ie
alanrogers.com/IR9370   www.camping.ie

Accommodation: ☑Pitch   ☑Mobile home/chalet   ☑Hotel/B&B   ☐ Apartment

Ballinacourty House and its cobble-stoned courtyard form the centrepiece of this south-facing park with views of the Galtee Mountains. Accessed by a tree-lined lane, the reception area is in part of the renovated 18th-century building, as is the adjoining restaurant. The park is level with 26 touring pitches with 6A electricity and 19 grassy pitches for tents. Some areas are shaded and there are open spaces to accommodate rallies and larger groups. Self-catering cottages and B&B are also available. This tranquil site is very appealing to families with young children. It is an excellent base from which to tour the Rock of Cashel, the Mitchelstown Caves, Swiss Cottage and the towns of Tipperary, Cahir and Cashel. Activities in the area include horse riding and trekking, fishing for perch and brown trout, cycling, forest walks, three 18-hole golf courses, leisure centre with swimming pool, cinema theatre and pottery shop.

You might like to know

There are a number of superb walking trails in the locality – very suitable for families with plenty of information panels on the flora and fauna of the area and picnic tables along the way. This corner of Ireland is also a haven for painters and photographers alike.

- ☑ Riding
- ☑ Pony trekking
- ☑ Tennis
- ☑ Mountain biking
- ☑ Sports field
- ☑ Outdoor pool
- ☑ Golf
- ☑ Hiking
- ☑ Go-karting
- ☑ Fishing

Facilities: Sanitary facilities provide free hot water and showers. Baby room. Laundry with ironing facilities. Campers' kitchen. Ice pack freezing. Licensed restaurant (early booking advised). Motorcaravan services. Gas supplies. Frisbee golf. TV and games rooms. Picnic benches. Tennis. Play area. Off site: Riding, fishing, golf within 5 miles.

Open: Easter - last Sunday in September.

Directions: Follow the N24 from Tipperary or Cahir to Bansha. Turn on to R663 for about 7 miles, passing Glen Hotel after 6 miles. Follow signs for Ballinacourty House. GPS: 52.41614, -8.21047

Charges guide

Per unit incl. 2 persons	€ 8,00 - € 10,00
extra person	€ 5,00
child	€ 2,00
electricity	€ 3,00

Fossa Caravan & Camping Park

Fossa, Killarney (Co. Kerry)
t: **064 663 1497** e: **fossaholidays@eircom.net**
alanrogers.com/IR9590 www.camping-holidaysireland.com/

Accommodation: ☑Pitch ☑Mobile home/chalet ☐Hotel/B&B ☐Apartment

This park is in the village of Fossa, ten minutes by car or bus (six per day) from Killarney town centre. Fossa Caravan Park has a distinctive reception building and hostel accommodation, a stimulating play area and shop. The park is divided in two – the touring caravan area lies to the right, tucked behind the main building and to the left is an open grass area, mainly for campers. Touring pitches with electricity (10/15A) and drainage have hardstanding and are angled between shrubs and trees in a garden setting. To the rear at a higher level and discreetly placed are 30 caravan holiday homes, sheltered by the thick foliage of the wooded slopes which climb high behind the park. Not only is Fossa convenient for Killarney (5.5 km.), it is also en-route for the famed Ring of Kerry, and makes an ideal base for walkers and golfers. Less than 8 km. away are the famous walk up the Gap of Dunloe, and Carrantuohill, the highest mountain in Ireland.

You might like to know
The Dingle Peninsula offers fantastic views and winding lanes through small villages down to Slea Head where you can see the Blasket Islands.

☑ Riding
☑ Pony trekking
☑ Tennis
☑ Cycling *(road)*
☑ Mountain biking
☑ Outdoor pool
☑ Golf
☑ Hiking
☑ Fishing
☑ Mountaineering

Facilities: Modern toilet facilities include showers on payment. En suite unit for campers with disabilities. Laundry room. Campers' kitchen. Shop. Takeaway (8/7-25/8). TV lounge. Tennis. Play area. Picnic area. Games room. Security patrol. Off site: Fishing and golf 2 km. Riding 3 km. Bicycle hire 5 km. Woodland walk into Killarney. A visit to Killarney National Park is highly recommended.

Open: 1 April - 30 September.

Directions: Approaching Killarney from all directions, follow signs for N72 Ring of Kerry and Killorglin. At last roundabout join R562/N72. Continue for 5.5 km. and Fossa is the second park to the right. GPS: 52.07071, -9.58573

Charges guide

Per unit incl. 2 persons and electricity	€ 24,00 - € 26,00
extra person	€ 6,00
child (under 14 yrs)	€ 2,50
hiker/cyclist incl. tent	€ 8,00 - € 9,00

IRELAND – Cahirciveen

Mannix Point Camping & Caravan Park

Cahirciveen (Co. Kerry)
t: 066 947 2806   e: mortimer@campinginkerry.com
alanrogers.com/IR9610   www.campinginkerry.com

Accommodation: ☑Pitch ☑Mobile home/chalet ☐ Hotel/B&B ☐ Apartment

A tranquil, beautifully located, seashore park, it is no exaggeration to describe Mannix Point as a nature lovers' paradise. Situated in one of the most spectacular parts of the Ring of Kerry, overlooking the bay and Valentia Island, the rustic seven-acre park commands splendid views in all directions. The park road meanders through the level site and offers 42 pitches of various sizes and shape, many with shelter and seclusion. There are 42 electrical connections (10A) available. A charming, old flower bedecked fisherman's cottage has been converted to provide facilities including reception, excellent campers' kitchen and a cosy sitting room with turf fire. There is no television, but compensation comes in the form of a knowledgeable, hospitable owner who is a Bord Fáilte registered local tour guide. The site opens directly onto marshland which teems with wildlife (a two acre nature reserve) with direct access to the beach and seashore. A viewing platform allows observation of seals and birdlife. This park is also an ideal resting place for people walking the Kerry Way.

Special offers
Please see www.campinginkerry.com for special offers which vary from time to time.

☑ Riding
☑ Pony trekking
☑ Crafts
☑ Diving
☑ Rock climbing
☑ Hiking
☑ Canoeing
☑ Kayaking
☑ Pedaloes
☑ Bird watching

☑ Skellig tours
☑ Foreshore walks
☑ Whale watching trips
☑ Amphibious cruises

You might like to know
Sailing, surfing, wind-surfing, water skiing. The Atlantic Sailing Club (dingies) operates from Mannix Point. Club member rates available to campers. Fishing. Fitness facilities. Cycling and mountain biking.

Facilities: Toilet and shower facilities were clean when we visited. Modern and well equipped campers' kitchen and dining area. Comfortable campers' sitting room. Laundry facilities with washing machines and dryer. Motorcaravan service point. Picnic and barbecue facilities. Fishing and boat launching from site.
Off site: Bicycle hire 800 m. Riding 3 km. Golf 14 km. Pubs, restaurants and shops 15 minutes walk. Watersports, bird watching, walking and photography. Local cruises to Skelligs Rock with free transport to and from the port for walkers and cyclists.

Open: 15 March - 15 October.

Directions: Park is 300 m. off the N70 Ring of Kerry road, 800 m. southwest of Cahirciveen (or Cahersiveen) on the road towards Waterville. GPS: 51.94281, -10.2434

Charges guide

Per unit incl. 2 persons and electricity	€ 27,00
extra person	€ 6,00

Reductions for activity groups and rallies if pre-paid. No credit cards.

BELGIUM – Jabbeke

Recreatiepark Klein Strand

Varsenareweg 29, B-8490 Jabbeke (West Flanders)
t: 050 811 440   e: info@kleinstrand.be
alanrogers.com/BE0555   www.kleinstrand.be

Accommodation: ☑Pitch ☑Mobile home/chalet ☐Hotel/B&B ☐Apartment

In a convenient location, just off the A10 motorway and close to Bruges, this site is in two distinct areas divided by an access road. The touring section has 137 large pitches on flat grass separated by well-trimmed hedges; all have electricity and access to water and drainage. Though surrounded by mobile homes and seasonal caravans, this is a surprisingly relaxing area and the ambience should be further enhanced in 2011 when a small park is to be created at its centre. Some children's leisure facilities are provided here, and there is a spacious bar and a snack bar with takeaway. The main site with all the privately-owned mobile homes is closer to the lake and this area has most of the amenities. These include the main reception building, restaurants, bar, minimarket, and sports facilities. This is a family holiday site and offers a comprehensive programme of activities and entertainment in July/August. The lake is used for water skiing and has a supervised swimming area with waterslides (high season) and a beach volleyball area.

You might like to know
There is a sports school where you can learn to water ski.

- ☑ Riding
- ☑ Tennis
- ☑ Cycling (road)
- ☑ Outdoor pool
- ☑ Water skiing
- ☑ Golf
- ☑ Paintball
- ☑ Beach volleyball
- ☑ Watersports
- ☑ Team building

Facilities: A single modern, heated, toilet block in the touring area provides the usual facilities including good sized showers (charged). Baby room. Basic facilities for disabled campers. Laundry. Motorcaravan service point. Bar and snack bar. Children's playground. Fun pool for small children. In main park: European and Chinese restaurants, bar and snack bar, takeaways (all year). Shop (Easter-end Aug). Tennis courts and sports field. Water ski school; water-ski shows (Sundays in July/Aug), Bicycle hire. Cable TV point (incl.) and Wifi (charged, first hour free) on all pitches. Off site: Riding 5 km. Beach 8 km. Golf and sailing 10 km.

Open: All year.

Directions: From A18/A10 motorways, take exit 6/6B signed Jabbeke. At roundabout take first exit signed for site. In 650 m on left-hand bend, turn left to site in 600 m. Main reception is on left but in high season continue to touring site on right in 200 m. GPS: 51.18448, 3.10445

Charges guide

Per unit incl. up to 6 persons and electricity	€ 17,00 - € 34,00
dog	€ 2,00

BELGIUM – Lichtaart

Camping Floreal Kempen

Herentalsesteenweg 64, B-2460 Lichtaart (Antwerp)
t: **014 556 120** e: **kempen@florealclub.be**
alanrogers.com/BE0665 **www.florealclub.be**

Accommodation: ☑Pitch ☑Mobile home/chalet ☐ Hotel/B&B ☐ Apartment

This is an attractive woodland site and is a member of the Floréal group. It is located close to the well known 'Purperen Heide', a superb nature reserve with 15 scenic footpaths leading through it. There are 207 pitches, of which only 26 are reserved for touring units. These are of a good size (100 m² or more), all with 10A electricity and most with their own water supply. Several simple cabins are available for hikers, as well as fully equipped mobile homes. There are some good leisure facilities, including tennis and a multisport pitch, as well as a popular bar and restaurant. Day trips to Antwerp are very much a possibility. The old city is a gem with a great deal of interest, including over a thousand noted monuments, a diamond museum and the Rubens trail. Another popular visit is to the charming Bobbejaanlaan amusement park. There are miles of forest trails and the site's friendly managers will be pleased to recommend routes.

You might like to know
During your holiday why not visit Bobbejaanland amusement park? It is just a few kilometres from the campsite.

- ☑ **Riding**
- ☑ **Tennis**
- ☑ **Cycling** (road)
- ☑ **Sports field**
- ☑ **Outdoor pool**
- ☑ **Golf**
- ☑ **Aerial walkways**
- ☑ **Football**
- ☑ **Basketball**
- ☑ **Sports terrain**
  (all-weather)

Facilities: Toilet facilities are in need of some investment. When we visited cleaning and maintenance needed attention. Motorcaravan services. Shop. Bar. Restaurant. Tennis. Play area. Multisport terrain. Tourist information. Mobile homes for rent. Off site: Walking and cycle tracks. Golf. Antwerp. Bobbejaanlaan amusement park

Open: All year.

Directions: Approaching from Antwerp, head east on A21 motorway as far as exit 24 (Turnhout). Leave here and head south on the N19 to Kasterlee, and then west on N123 to Lichtaart. Follow signs to the site.
GPS: 51.21024, 4.90423

Charges guide

Per unit incl. 2 persons	€ 11,00 - € 16,50
extra person	€ 3,25
child (3-11 yrs)	€ 2,50
dog (max. 1)	€ 3,00

NETHERLANDS – Wolphaartsdijk

Camping De Veerhoeve

Veerweg 48, NL-4471 NC Wolphaartsdijk (Zeeland)
t: **0113 581 155** e: **info@deveerhoeve.nl**
alanrogers.com/NL5580 **www.deveerhoeve.nl**

Accommodation: ☑Pitch ☑Mobile home/chalet ☐ Hotel/B&B ☐ Apartment

This is a family-run site near the shores of the Veerse Meer which is ideal for family holidays. It is situated in a popular area for watersports and is well suited for sailing, windsurfing or fishing enthusiasts, with boat launching 100 m. away. A sandy beach and recreation area ideal for children is only a five minute walk. As with most sites in this area there are many mature static and seasonal pitches. However, part of the friendly, relaxed site is reserved for touring units with 90 marked pitches on grassy ground, all with electrical connections. A member of the Holland Tulip Parcs group.

You might like to know
Why not take a trip on the historic steam train? It is great fun for the children!
Or maybe a visit to Miniature Walcheren the Delta Expo or the fish auction at Colijnsplaat.

- ☑ Riding
- ☑ Tennis
- ☑ Cycling *(road)*
- ☑ Sailing
- ☑ Surfing
- ☑ Windsurfing
- ☑ Golf
- ☑ Hiking
- ☑ Canoeing
- ☑ Fishing

Facilities: Sanitary facilities in three blocks have been well modernised with full tiling. Hot showers are on payment. Laundry facilities. Motorcaravan services. Supermarket (all season). Restaurant and snack bar. TV room. Tennis. Playground and play field. Games room. Bicycle hire. Fishing. Accommodation for groups. Max. 1 dog. WiFi. Off site: Slipway for launching boats 100 m. Riding 2 km. Golf 5 km.

Open: 1 April - 30 October.

Directions: From N256 Goes - Zierikzee road take Wolphaartsdijk exit. Follow through village and signs to site (be aware - one of the site signs is obscured by other road signs and could be missed). GPS: 51.54678, 3.81345

Charges guide

Per unit incl. 1-4 persons	€ 21,50 - € 24,50
incl. electricity (6A), water and drainage	€ 22,50 - € 25,50
incl. TV connection	€ 24,00 - € 27,50

NETHERLANDS – Uitdam

Camping Jachthaven Uitdam

Zeedijk 2, NL-1154 PP Uitdam (Noord-Holland)
t: **0204 031 433** e: **info@campinguitdam.nl**
alanrogers.com/NL5720 www.campinguitdam.nl

Accommodation: ☑Pitch ☑Mobile home/chalet ☐ Hotel/B&B ☐ Apartment

Situated beside the Markermeer which is used extensively for watersports, this large site has its own private yachting marina (300 yachts and boats). It has 200 seasonal and permanent pitches, many used by watersports enthusiasts, but also offers 260 marked tourist pitches (180 with 4/6A electricity) on open, grassy ground overlooking the water and 24 mobile homes to rent. There is a special area for campers with bicycles. Very much dominated by the marina, this site will appeal to watersports enthusiasts, with opportunities for sailing, windsurfing and swimming, or for fishing, but it is also on a pretty stretch of coast. All the touring pitches have been upgraded with new drainage and there are new cabins for rent. Uitdam is 15 km. northeast of Amsterdam and is close to the ancient, small towns of Marken, Volendam and Monnickendam, which are well worth a visit. The views over the IJsselmeer from both ends of the touring fields are wonderful and this alone makes this site well worth visiting.

You might like to know
Camping Jachthaven Uitdam can be found on the edge of the protected 'Waterland' nature area. These surroundings are the perfect place for cycling, boating or just hiking.

- ☑ **Tennis**
- ☑ **Cycling** *(road)*
- ☑ **Sports field**
- ☑ **Sailing**
- ☑ **Windsurfing**
- ☑ **Golf**
- ☑ **Hiking**
- ☑ **Canoeing**
- ☑ **Fishing**
- ☑ **Children's pool**

Facilities: Two good toilet blocks and one rather basic toilet block with toilets only. Good facilities include hot showers on payment, toilets, washbasins and a baby room. Motorcaravan services. Gas supplies. Shop (1/4-1/10). Bar/restaurant (weekends and high season). TV room. Tennis. Playground and paddling pool. Bicycle hire. Fishing. Yacht marina (with fuel) and slipway. Watersports. Entertainment in high season. Off site: Riding 4 km. Sailing 6 km. Golf 12 km.

Open: 1 March - 1 November.

Directions: From the A10, take exit S116 onto the N247 towards Volendam. Then take Monnickendam exit south in direction of Marken on N518, then Uitdam. Site is just outside Uitdam. GPS: 52.42780, 5.07347

Charges guide

Per unit incl. 2 persons	€ 22,50
tent incl. 2 persons	€ 15,50 - € 19,00
extra person (over 3 yrs)	€ 3,00
boat on trailer	€ 7,00

NETHERLANDS – Vledder

Recreatiecentrum De Adelhof

Vledderweg 19, NL-8381 AB Vledder (Drenthe)
t: 0521 381 440   e: info@adelhof.nl
alanrogers.com/NL6125   www.adelhof.nl

Accommodation: ☑Pitch ☑Mobile home/chalet ☐Hotel/B&B ☐Apartment

With a fine location close to the large nature reserves of the Drents Friese Wold and Het Land van Oost, Recreatiecentrum De Adelhof is an ideal base for a cycling holiday in Drenthe, with miles of cycle tracks in the area. This is also a good site for anglers with a well stocked fishing lake. On site, there is a lively activity programme in high season. Activities include craft work, treasure hunts, theatre and musical evenings. The café/restaurant is the focal point here and is also the location for musical evenings. Here you can also play billiards, darts or watch TV. De Adelhof has 200 spacious touring pitches spread over several fields. The pitches are surrounded by bushes and shrubs to ensure privacy. They are generally around 100 m² and all have electricity. Several attractive children's play areas have been created in each of the fields. One field in particular is reserved for families with dogs. There are also chalets available for rent.

Special offers
At Ascension, Whitsun and for six weeks in high season, a professional programme of recreational activities is offered.

You might like to know
There are several beautiful cycle and walking trails in the park. Fishing is available in the large central pond. The park includes a café, restaurant, snack-bar, camping shop and several playgrounds.

☑ Riding
☑ Pony trekking
☑ Tennis
☑ Cycling (road)
☑ Sports field
☑ Outdoor pool
☑ Hiking
☑ 10-pin bowling
☑ Fishing
☑ Table tennis

☑ Minigolf
☑ Cycle hire
☑ Go-kart rental

Facilities: Four toilet blocks with all the usual facilities (one is open in the winter). Small shop (end April-end Aug). Café/restaurant and snack bar (April-Nov). Large fishing lake with carp. Children's farm. Play areas. All-weather tennis. Minigolf. Bicycle and go-kart hire. Football field. Volleyball. Table tennis. Professional entertainment team (spring holidays and high season). Off site: Municipal outdoor swimming pool (end April-beginning Sept, fee charged). Cycle and walking trails. Miramar Museum. 'Speelstad Oranje' adventure park. Dwingelerveld national park. Nearby towns of Steenwijk, Meppel, Assen and Heerenveen.

Open: All year.

Directions: Vledder is 10 km. northeast of Steenwijk. From A38 motorway take the Steenwijk exit and follow N855 north to Frederiksoord and Vledder. The site is just before the village to the right. GPS: 52.85178, 6.19845

Charges guide

Per unit incl. 2 persons and electricity	€ 23,00

90

Camping De Schatberg

Midden Peelweg 5, NL-5975 MZ Sevenum (Limburg)
t: **0774 677 777** e: **info@schatberg.nl**
alanrogers.com/NL6510 www.schatberg.nl

Accommodation: ☑Pitch ☑Mobile home/chalet ☐ Hotel/B&B ☐ Apartment

In a woodland setting of 86 hectares, this family run campsite is more reminiscent of a holiday village, with a superb range of activities that makes it an ideal venue for families. Look out for the deer! A large site with 1,100 pitches and many mobile homes and seasonal or weekend visitors, there are 500 touring pitches. All have electricity (6,10,16A), cable, water and drainage and average 100-150 m² in size. They are on rough grass terrain, mostly with shade, but not separated. Forty pitches have private sanitary facilities (two with sauna and jacuzzi). Road noise can be heard in some areas of this large campsite. The surrounding countryside offers the opportunity to enjoy nature, either by cycling or walking. For the more 'stay on site' visitor the location is excellent with several lakes for fishing, windsurfing and swimming, plus an extensive range of activities and a heated outdoor pool. A feature at De Schatberg is the attractive restaurant/bar area and the reception and indoor pool, manned by friendly staff.

You might like to know
At the entrance is a natural pool with sandy beach, a sunbathing area, a small port and several playgrounds. A little further on is the surfing and fishing lake.

☑ **Cycling** *(road)*
☑ **Sports field**
☑ **Outdoor pool**
☑ **Windsurfing**
☑ **Golf**
☑ **Aerial walkways**
☑ **10-pin bowling**
☑ **Fishing**
☑ **Trampolining**

Facilities: Five modern, fully equipped toilet blocks, supplemented by three small wooden toilet units to save night time walks, receive heavy use in high season and maintenance can be variable. Family shower rooms, baby baths and en-suite units for disabled visitors. Washing machines and dryers. Motorcaravan service point. Supermarket. Restaurant, bar and takeaway. Pizzeria. Pancake restaurant. Indoor and outdoor pools. Trampoline. Play areas. Fishing. Watersports. Bicycle hire. Games room. Bowling, casino and underground disco. Entertainment in high season. Max. 1 dog. Off site: Golf 0.5 km.

Open: All year.

Directions: Site is 8 km. west-northwest of Venlo. Leave the A67 Eindhoven - Venlo motorway at Helden, exit 38. Travel north on the 277 for 500 m. and site is signed at new roundabout. GPS: 51.382964, 5.976147

Charges guide

Per unit incl. 1-4 persons and electricity	€ 21,50 - € 52,50

Camping BreeBronne

Lange Heide 9, NL-5993 PB Maasbree (Limburg)
t: **0774 652 360** e: **info@breebronne.nl**
alanrogers.com/NL6520 **www.breebronne.nl**

Accommodation: ☑Pitch ☑Mobile home/chalet ☐Hotel/B&B ☐Apartment

One of the top campsites in the Netherlands, BreeBronne is set around a large lake in a forest region. There are 370 pitches, of which 220 are for touring units. These are at least 100 m² in size and all have electricity (10A), water, waste water and cable TV connections. The touring pitches are placed in separate areas from the static units and some pitch areas are kept for people with dogs. The lake provides a sandy beach with a water slide and opportunities for swimming, sailing and windsurfing. Alternatively, you can swim in the heated open air pool or the 'sub-tropical' heated indoor pool with its special children's area. Possible excursions from the site might include a visit to Arcen, beside the Maas river, with its Schloss garden and the nearby naturally heated thermal bath. There are boat trips on the Maas. Shopping in Venlo is good with its Saturday morning market. Member of Leading Campings Group.

You might like to know

You may wish to visit the castle ruins of Arcen, the De Groote Peel National Park and the De Hamert National Park – all within a distance of 15 km.

- ☑ Riding
- ☑ Tennis
- ☑ Mountain biking
- ☑ Outdoor pool
- ☑ Archery
- ☑ Sailing
- ☑ Windsurfing
- ☑ Golf
- ☑ Hiking
- ☑ Fishing

Facilities: The sanitary facilities are top class with a special section for children, decorated in fairy tale style, and excellent provision for disabled visitors and seniors. Launderette. Dog shower. Solarium. Private bathrooms for hire. Shop (1/4-31/10). Bar and 'De Bron' restaurant with regional specialities (all year). Takeaway. Outdoor swimming pool (15/5-1/10). Indoor pool with area for children (all year). Play area. Play room. Internet. Tennis. Animation. Fishing. Bicycle hire. Max. 1 dog. Off site: Fishing 2 km. Golf and riding 5 km. Walking in the National Parks.

Open: All year.

Directions: BreeBronne is 8 km. west of Venlo. From autobahn A67 towards Eindhoven take exit 38 and head south on the 277 road. After 3 km. fork right for Maasbree, then left (Maasbree) on the 275. At roundabout in Maasbree take third exit (site signed). Go through town and turn right after 2 km. to site 1 km. on left. GPS: 51.36665, 6.04166

Charges guide

Per unit incl. 4 persons	€ 28,50 - € 46,60
extra person	€ 4,90
dog	€ 5,50
private bathroom	€ 12,00

Kennemer Duincamping De Lakens

Zeeweg 60, NL-2051 EC Bloemendaal aan Zee (Noord-Holland)
t: **0235 411 570** e: **delakens@kennemerduincampings.nl**
alanrogers.com/NL6870 www.kennemerduincampings.nl

Accommodation: ☑Pitch ☑Mobile home/chalet ☐ Hotel/B&B ☐ Apartment

De Lakens is part of de Kennemer Duincampings group and is beautifully located in the dunes at Bloemendaal aan Zee. This site has 940 reasonably large, flat pitches with a hardstanding of shells. There are 410 for touring units (235 with 16A electricity) and the sunny pitches are separated by low hedging. This site is a true oasis of peace in a part of the Netherlands usually bustling with activity. From this site it is possible to walk straight through the dunes to the North Sea. Although there is no pool, there is the sea. A separate area is provided for groups and youngsters to maintain the quiet atmosphere. It is not far to Amsterdam or Alkmaar and its cheese market. We feel you could have an enjoyable holiday here.

You might like to know

Activities are organised for children and there is a playing area for them on the beach including a pirate ship. There is a golf course 10 km. from the site.

☑ **Cycling** *(road)*
☑ **Crafts**
☑ **Surfing**
☑ **Hiking**
☑ **Sea swimming**
☑ **Basketball**
☑ **Volleyball**
☑ **Table tennis**
☑ **Kite flying**

Facilities: The six toilet blocks for tourers (two brand new) include controllable showers, washbasins (open style and in cabins), facilities for disabled people and a baby room. Launderette. Two motorcaravan service points. Bar/restaurant and snack bar. Supermarket. Adventure playgrounds. Bicycle hire. Entertainment program in high season for all. Dogs are not accepted. Off site: Beach and riding 1 km. Golf 10 km.

Open: 20 March - 1 November.

Directions: From Amsterdam go west to Haarlem and follow the N200 from Haarlem towards Bloemendaal aan Zee. Site is on the N200, on the right hand side.
GPS: 52.40563, 4.58652

Charges guide

Per unit incl. 4 persons	€ 14,10 - € 27,45
incl. electricity	€ 18,40 - € 28,70
extra person	€ 4,20

GERMANY – Wulfen

Camping Wulfener Hals

Wulfener Hals Weg, D-23769 Wulfen auf Fehmarn (Schleswig-Holstein)
t: 043 718 6280 e: camping@wulfenerhals.de
alanrogers.com/DE3003 www.wulfenerhals.de

Accommodation: ☑Pitch ☑Mobile home/chalet ☐Hotel/B&B ☐Apartment

If you are travelling to Denmark or on to Sweden, taking the E47/A1 then B207 from Hamburg, and the ferry from Puttgarden to Rødbyhavn, this is a top class all year round site, either to rest overnight or as a base for a longer stay. Attractively situated by the sea, it is a large, mature site (34 hectares) and is well maintained. It has over 800 individual pitches of up to 160 m² (half for touring) in glades with some separated by bushes, with shade in the older parts, less in the newer areas nearer the sea. There are many hardstandings and 552 pitches have electricity, water and drainage. A separate area is for motorcaravans. The site provides 60 extra large pitches, all with electricity, water and drainage, and some with TV aerial points, together with a new toilet block. There is much to do for young and old alike at Wulfener Hals, with a new heated outdoor pool and paddling pool (unsupervised), although the sea is naturally popular as well. The site also has many sporting facilities including its own golf courses and schools for watersports. Member of Leading Campings Group.

Special offers
Swimming lessons for children.

You might like to know
You may be interested in watching or even participating in the Surf and Kite Festival on the island of Fehmarn.

☑ Riding
☑ Mountain biking
☑ Archery
☑ Sailing
☑ Surfing
☑ Windsurfing
☑ Kitesurfing
☑ Diving
☑ Waterskiing
☑ Fishing

Facilities: Five heated sanitary buildings have first class facilities including showers and both open washbasins and private cabins. Family bathrooms for rent. Facilities for disabled people. Laundry. Motorcaravan services. Shop, bar, restaurants and takeaway (April-Oct). Swimming pool (May-Oct). Sauna. Solarium. Jacuzzi. Sailing, windsurfing and diving schools. Boat slipway. Golf courses (18 hole, par 72 and 9 hole, par 27). Riding. Fishing. Archery. Good play equipment for younger children. Bicycle hire. Catamaran hire. Off site: Naturist beach 500 m. Village minimarket 2 km.

Open: All year.

Directions: From Hamburg take A1/E47 north to Puttgarden, cross the bridge onto the island of Fehmarn and turn right twice to Avendorf and follow the signs for Wulfen and the site. GPS: 54.40805, 11.17374

Charges guide

Per unit incl. 2 persons and electricity	€ 13,30 - € 44,40
extra person	€ 3,90 - € 8,40
child (2-13 yrs)	€ 2,30 - € 5,70
child (14-18 yrs)	€ 3,40 - € 7,30

Plus surcharges for larger pitches.
Many discounts and special family prices.

GERMANY – Wesel

Erholungszentrum Grav-Insel

Grav-Insel 1, D-46487 Wesel (North Rhine-Westphalia)
t: 028 197 2830   e: info@grav-insel.com
alanrogers.com/DE3202   www.grav-insel.de

Accommodation: ☑Pitch ☑Mobile home/chalet ☐ Hotel/B&B ☐ Apartment

Grav-Insel claims to be the largest family camping site in Germany, providing entertainment and activities to match, with over 2,000 permanent units. A section for 500 touring units runs beside the water to the left of the entrance and this area has been completely renewed. These pitches, all with 10A electricity, are flat, grassy, mostly without shade and of about 100 m². A walk through the site takes you past a nature reserve and to the Rhine where you can watch the barges. Despite its size, this site is very well maintained, calm, clean and spacious and this is down to the family which started it 40 years ago. This site, on the border with Holland, is an excellent stop over for the north and east of Germany. However, once here, you may decide to stay longer to take advantage of the excellent restaurant (special evenings each week), bird watching on the private reserve or to visit Xanten with its Roman amphitheatre in the archaeological park.

You might like to know

If you are looking for recreation, an exciting experience, education ans fun – the Duisburg-Nord Landscape Park is all you need.

- ☑ **Cycling** *(road)*
- ☑ **Sports field**
- ☑ **Outdoor pool**
- ☑ **Sailing**
- ☑ **Hiking**
- ☑ **Fishing**
- ☑ **Football**
- ☑ **Children's zoo**
- ☑ **Beach volleyball**
- ☑ **Motor boats**

Facilities: Excellent sanitary facilities, all housed in a modern building above which is the bar/restaurant (open all year). Touring area augmented by portacabin units to be renewed. Facilities for disabled visitors. Baby room. Launderette. Motorcaravan service point. Large supermarket. Entertainment area with satellite TV. WiFi. Solarium. Large play area on sand plus wet weather indoor area. Boat park. Sailing. Fishing. Swimming. Football (international coaching in high season). Animation in high season. Off site: Bus service 500 m.

Open: All year.

Directions: Site is 5 km. northwest of Wesel. From the A3 take exit 6 and B58 towards Wesel, then right towards Rees. Turn left at sign for Flüren, through Flüren and left to site after 1.5 km. If approaching Wesel from the west (B58), cross the Rhine, turn left at first traffic lights and follow signs Grav-Insel and Flüren. GPS: 51.67062, 6.55600

Charges guide

Per person	€ 2,00 - € 3,00
child (under 12 yrs)	€ 1,00 - € 1,50
pitch incl. electricity	€ 6,00 - € 9,50
dog	€ 0,50 - € 1,00

Camping & Ferienpark Teichmann

Zum Träumen 1A, D-34516 Vöhl-Herzhausen (Hessen)
t: 056 352 45 e: camping-teichmann@t-online.de
alanrogers.com/DE3280 www.camping-teichmann.de

Accommodation: ☑ Pitch ☑ Mobile home/chalet ☐ Hotel/B&B ☐ Apartment

Situated near the eastern end of the 27 km. long Edersee and the National Park Kellerwald-Edersee, this attractively set site is surrounded by wooded hills and encircles a six hectare lake which has separate areas for swimming, fishing and boating. Of the 460 pitches 250 are touring, all with 10A electricity and 50 with fresh and waste water connections. The pitches are on level grass, some having an area of hardstanding, and are separated by hedges and mature trees. At the far side of the lake from the entrance is a separate area for tents with its own sanitary block. The adjoining national park, a popular leisure region, offers a wealth of holiday/sporting activities including walking, cycling, (there are two passenger ferries that take cycles), boat trips, cable car and much more. For winter sport lovers the ski centre at Winterberg is only 30 km. away from this all year round site. With a wide range of facilities for children, this is an ideal family site as well as being suited to country lovers who can enjoy the endless forest and lakeside walks/cycle tracks in the park.

You might like to know

This site is open all year and is just 30 km. from the winter sport centre at Winterberg.

- ☑ Riding
- ☑ Tennis
- ☑ Cycling (road)
- ☑ Golf
- ☑ Hiking
- ☑ Skiing (downhill)
- ☑ Canoeing
- ☑ Fishing
- ☑ Cable car

Facilities: Three good quality sanitary blocks can be heated and have free showers, washbasins (open and in cabins), baby rooms and facilities for wheelchair users. Laundry. Motorcaravan services. Café and shop (both summer only). Restaurant by entrance open all day (closed Feb). Watersports. Boat and bicycle hire. Lake swimming. Fishing. Minigolf. Tennis. Playground. Sauna. Solarium. Disco (high season). Internet access. Off site: New National Park opposite site entrance. Riding 500 m. Golf 25 km. Cable car (you can take bikes). Aquapark. Boat trips on the Edersee.

Open: All year.

Directions: Site is 45 km. from Kassel. From A44 Oberhausen - Kassel autobahn, take exit 64 for Diemelstadt and head south for Korbach. Site is between Korbach and Frankenberg on the B252 road, 1 km. to the south of Herzhausen at the pedestrian traffic lights.
GPS: 51.17550, 8.89067

Charges guide

Per unit incl. 2 persons and electricity	€ 25,00 - € 29,00

GERMANY – Neuenburg

Gugel's Dreiländer Camping

Oberer Wald 3, D-79395 Neuenburg-am-Rhein (Baden-Württemberg)
t: **076 317 719** e: **info@camping-gugel.de**
alanrogers.com/DE3455 www.camping-gugel.de

Accommodation: ☑Pitch ☑Mobile home/chalet ☐ Hotel/B&B ☐ Apartment

Set in natural heath and woodland, Gugel's is an attractive site with 220 touring pitches either in small clearings in the trees, in open areas or on a hardstanding section used for single night stays. All have electricity (16A), and some also have water, waste water and satellite TV connections. Opposite is a meadow where late arrivals and early departures may spend the night. There may be some road noise near the entrance. The site may become very busy in high season and at Bank Holidays, but you should always find room. The excellent pool and wellness complex add to the attraction of this all year site. There is a social room with satellite TV where guests are welcomed with a glass of wine and a slide presentation of the attractions of the area. The Rhine is within walking distance. Neuenburg is ideally placed not only for enjoying and exploring the south of the Black Forest, but also for night stops when travelling from Frankfurt to Basel on the A5 autobahn. The permanent caravans set away from the tourist area, with their well-tended gardens, enhance rather than detract from the natural beauty.

You might like to know
Basel, Freiburg, Colmar, Breisach: these old towns with their minsters and cathedrals, the rich seats of the arts and their modern shopping quarters, can be enjoyed in an afternoon trip.

- ☑ Riding
- ☑ Tennis
- ☑ Cycling (road)
- ☑ Sports field
- ☑ Golf
- ☑ Fitness/gym
- ☑ Fishing
- ☑ Beach volleyball
- ☑ Nordic walking

Facilities: Three good quality heated sanitary blocks include some washbasins in cabins. Baby room. Facilities for disabled visitors. Laundry facilities. Motorcaravan services. Shop. Excellent restaurant. Takeaway (weekends and daily in high season). Wellness centre. Indoor/outdoor pool. Boules. Tennis. Fishing. Minigolf. Barbecue. Beach bar. Bicycle hire. Community room with TV. Activity programme (high season). Play areas. Off site: Riding 1.5 km. Golf 5 km. Neuenburg, Breisach, Freiburg, Basel and the Black Forest.

Open: All year.

Directions: From autobahn A5 take Neuenburg exit, turn left, then almost immediately left at traffic lights, left at next junction and follow signs for 2 km. to site (called 'Neuenburg' on most signs). GPS: 47.79693, 7.55000

Charges guide

Per unit incl. 2 persons and electricity	€ 22,00 - € 26,50
extra person	€ 6,50
child (2-15 yrs)	€ 3,00
dog	€ 3,00

GERMANY – Krün-Obb

Alpen-Caravanpark Tennsee

D-82494 Krün-Obb (Bavaria (S))
t: 088 251 70 e: info@camping-tennsee.de
alanrogers.com/DE3680 www.camping-tennsee.de

Accommodation: ☑Pitch ☑Mobile home/chalet ☐ Hotel/B&B ☐ Apartment

Tennsee is an excellent, friendly site in truly beautiful surroundings, high up (1,000 m) in the Karwendel Alps with super mountain views, and close to many famous places of which Innsbruck (44 km) and Oberammergau (26 km) are two. Mountain walks are plentiful, with several lifts close by. It is an attractive site with good facilities including 164 serviced pitches with individual connections for electricity (up to 16A and two connections), gas, TV, radio, telephone, water and waste water. The other 80 pitches all have electricity and some of these are available for overnight guests at a reduced rate. Reception and comfortable restaurants, bar, cellar youth room and a well stocked shop are all housed in attractive buildings. Many activities and excursions are organised to local attractions by the Zick family, who run the site in a very friendly, helpful and efficient manner.

You might like to know
There is a wonderful view of the Isar Valley and the Alpine scenery beyond from the mountain station of the nearby cable car.

- ☑ Riding
- ☑ Tennis
- ☑ Archery
- ☑ Sailing
- ☑ Windsurfing
- ☑ Diving
- ☑ Golf
- ☑ Skiing (downhill)
- ☑ Fishing
- ☑ Paragliding

Facilities: The first class toilet block has under-floor heating, washbasins in cabins and private units with WC, shower, basin and bidet for rent. Unit for disabled people with the latest facilities. Baby bath, dog bathroom and a heated room for ski equipment (with lockers). Washing machines, free dryers and irons. Gas supplies. Motorcaravan services. Cooking facilities. Shop. Restaurants (waiter, self service and takeaway). Bar. Youth room. Solarium. Bicycle hire. Playground. WiFi. Organised activities and excursions. Bus service to ski slopes in winter. Off site: Fishing 400 m. Riding and golf 3 km.

Open: All year excl. 6 November - 15 December.

Directions: Site is just off main Garmisch-Partenkirchen - Innsbruck road no. 2 between Klais and Krün, 15 km. from Garmisch watch for small sign 'Tennsee + Barmsee' and turn right there for site. GPS: 47.49066, 11.25396

Charges guide

Per unit incl. 2 persons	€ 27,00 - € 29,50
extra person	€ 9,25 - € 9,75
child (6-16 yrs)	€ 3,00 - € 4,00
electricity (per kWh)	€ 0,70
dog	€ 3,30

Camping Havelberge am Woblitzsee

An de Havelberg 1, D-17237 Userin/Ot Gross Quassau (Mecklenburg-West Pomerania)
t: 039 812 4790 e: info@haveltourist.de
alanrogers.com/DE3820 www.haveltourist.de

Accommodation: ☑Pitch ☑Mobile home/chalet ☐ Hotel/B&B ☐ Apartment

The Müritz National Park is a very large area of lakes and marshes, popular for birdwatching as well as watersports, and Havelberge is a large, well equipped site to use as a base for enjoying the area. It is quite steep in places here with many terraces, most with shade, less in newer areas, with views over the lake. There are 400 pitches in total with 330 good sized, numbered touring pitches, most with 16A electrical connections, and 230 pitches on a newly developed area to the rear of the site with water and drainage. Pitches on the new field are level and separated by low hedges and bushes but have no shade. Over 170 seasonal pitches with a number of attractive chalets and an equal number of mobile homes, are in a separate areas. In the high season this is a busy park with lots going on to entertain families of all ages, whilst in the low seasons this is a peaceful base for exploring an unspoilt area of nature. Member of Leading Campings Group.

You might like to know

Canoes available for hire (Canadian style or kayaks) and rowing boats. For beginners there are introductory canoeing courses.

- ☑ Riding
- ☑ Cycling (road)
- ☑ Mountain biking
- ☑ Crafts
- ☑ Sailing
- ☑ Waterskiing
- ☑ Hiking
- ☑ Aerial walkways
- ☑ Canoeing
- ☑ Fishing

Facilities: Four sanitary buildings (one new and of a very high standard) provide very good facilities, with private cabins, showers on payment and large section for children. Fully equipped kitchen and laundry. Motorcaravan service point. Small shop and modern restaurant (April-Oct). The lake provides fishing, swimming from a small beach and boats can be launched (over 5 hp requires a German boat licence). Canoes, rowing boats, windsurfers and bikes can be hired. Play areas and entertainment in high season. Internet access. Off site: Riding 3.5 km.

Open: All year.

Directions: From A19 Rostock - Berlin road take exit 18 and follow B198 to Wesenberg and go left to Klein Quassow and follow site signs. GPS: 53.30517, 13.00133

Charges guide

Per unit incl. 2 persons and electricity	€ 15,30 - € 31,50
extra person	€ 4,00 - € 6,50
child (2-14 yrs)	€ 1,50 - € 4,30
dog	€ 1,00 - € 4,30

CZECH REPUBLIC – Vrchlabi

Holiday Park Lisci Farma

Dolni Branna 350, CZ-54362 Vrchlabi (Vychodocesky)
t: 499 421 473 e: info@liscifarma.cz
alanrogers.com/CZ4590 www.liscifarma.cz

Accommodation: ☑Pitch ☑Mobile home/chalet ☐Hotel/B&B ☐Apartment

This is truly an excellent site that could be in Western Europe considering its amenities, pitches and welcome. However, Lisci Farma retains a pleasant Czech atmosphere. In the winter months, when local skiing is available, snow chains are essential. The 260 pitches are fairly flat, although the terrain is slightly sloping and some pitches are terraced. There is shade and some pitches have harstanding. The site is well equipped for the whole family to enjoy with its adventure playground offering trampolines for children, archery, beach volleyball, Russian bowling and an outdoor bowling court for older youngsters. A beautiful sandy, lakeside beach is 800 m. from the entrance. The more active amongst you can go paragliding or rock climbing, with experienced people to guide you. This site is very suitable for relaxing or exploring the culture of the area. Excursions to Prague are organised and, if all the sporting possibilities are not enough, the children can take part in the activities of the entertainment team.

You might like to know
There is an excellent restaurant on site, specialising in traditional Bohemian cuisine.

- ☑ Riding
- ☑ Tennis
- ☑ Cycling (road)
- ☑ Mountain biking
- ☑ Archery
- ☑ Sailing
- ☑ Rock climbing
- ☑ Hiking
- ☑ Fishing
- ☑ Paragliding

Facilities: Two good sanitary blocks, one near the entrance and another modern block next to the hotel, both include toilets, washbasins and spacious, controllable showers (on payment). Child size toilets and baby room. Toilet for disabled visitors. Sauna and massage. Launderette with sinks, hot water and a washing machine. Shop (15/6-15/9). Bar/snack bar with pool table. Games room. Swimming pool (6x12 m). Adventure style playground on grass with climbing wall. Trampolines. Tennis. Minigolf. Archery. Russian bowling. Paragliding. Rock climbing. Bicycle hire. Animation programme. Excursions to Prague. Off site: Fishing and beach 800 m. Riding 2 km. Golf 5 km.

Open: 1 December - 31 March and 1 May - 31 October.

Directions: Follow road no. 14 from Liberec to Vrchlabi. At the roundabout turn in the direction of Prague and site is about 1 mile on the right. GPS: 50.61036, 15.60264

Charges guide

Per unit incl. 2 persons and electricity	CZK 417 - 800
extra person	CZK 75 - 115
child (5-12 yrs)	CZK 59 - 90
dog	CZK 59 - 90

CZECH REPUBLIC – Frymburk

Camping Frymburk

Frymburk 184, CZ-38279 Frymburk (Jihocesky)
t: **380 735 284** e: **info@campingfrymburk.cz**
alanrogers.com/CZ4720 www.campingfrymburk.cz

Accommodation: ☑Pitch ☑Mobile home/chalet ☐Hotel/B&B ☐Apartment

Camping Frymburk is beautifully located on the Lipno lake in southern Bohemia and is
an ideal site. From this site, activities could include walking, cycling, swimming, sailing,
canoeing or rowing and afterwards you could relax in the small, cosy bar/restaurant.
You could enjoy a real Czech meal in one of the restaurants in Frymburk or on site.
The site has 170 level pitches on terraces (all with 6A electricity, some with hardstanding
and 4 have private sanitary units) and from the lower terraces on the edge of the lake
there are lovely views over the water to the woods on the opposite side. A ferry crosses
the lake from Frymburk where one can walk or cycle in the woods. The Dutch owner,
Mr Wilzing, will welcome the whole family, personally siting your caravan. Children will
be entertained by 'Kidstown' and the site has a small beach.

You might like to know
South Bohemia is the largest protected natural
area in the Czech Republic with an impressive
mountain range over 120 km. long.

☑ **Cycling** (road)
☑ **Mountain biking**
☑ **Crafts**
☑ **Windsurfing**
☑ **Rafting**
☑ **Hiking**
☑ **Canoeing**
☑ **Fishing**
☑ **Volleyball**

Facilities: Three immaculate toilet blocks with
toilets, washbasins, preset showers on payment
and an en-suite bathroom with toilet, basin
and shower. Facilities for disabled visitors.
Launderette. Restaurant and bar (10/5-15/9).
Motorcaravan services. Playground. Canoe,
bicycle, pedalos, rowing boat and surfboard hire.
Kidstown. Volleyball competitions. Rafting. Bus
trips to Prague. Torches useful. Internet access
and WiFi. Off site: Village 900 m. from reception.
Golf 7 km. Riding 20 km.

Open: 30 April - 1 October.

Directions: Take exit 114 at Passau in Germany
(near the Austrian border) towards Freyung in
the Czech Republic. Continue on this road till
Philipsreut and from there follow the no. 4 road
towards Vimperk. Turn right after the border
towards Volary on no. 141 road. From Volary
follow the no. 163 road to Horni Plana, Cerna
and Frymburk. Site is on the 163 road, right after
the village. GPS: 48.655947, 14.170239

Charges guide

Per unit incl. 2 persons and electricity	CZK 460 - 620
extra person	CZK 70 - 100
child (under 12 yrs)	CZK 50 - 70

No credit cards.

CZECH REPUBLIC – Nové Straseci

Camping Bucek

Tratice 170, CZ-27101 Nové Straseci (Stredocesky)
t: **313 564 212** e: **info@campingbucek.cz**
alanrogers.com/CZ4825 www.campingbucek.cz

Accommodation: ☑Pitch ☑Mobile home/chalet ☐ Hotel/B&B ☐ Apartment

Camping Bucek is a pleasant, Dutch owned site 40 km. west of Prague. Its proprietors also own Camping Frymburk (CZ4720). Bucek is located on the edge of woodland and has direct access to a small lake – canoes and rowing boats are available for hire, as well as sun loungers on the site's private beach. There are 100 pitches here, many with pleasant views over the lake, and all with electrical connections (6A). Shade is quite limited. Nearby, Revnicov is a pleasant small town with a range of shops and restaurants. The castles of Karlstejn and Krivoklát are also within easy access, along with Karlovy Vary and Prague itself.

You might like to know
Prague is within easy reach, just 40 km. away.

- ☑ Riding
- ☑ Cycling *(road)*
- ☑ Mountain biking
- ☑ Crafts
- ☑ Windsurfing
- ☑ Hiking
- ☑ Canoeing
- ☑ Fishing

Facilities: Renovated toilet blocks with free hot showers. Washing and drying machine. Direct lake access. Swimming pool. Pedaloes, canoes, lounger hire. Minigolf. Play area. Off site: Revnicov 2 km. with shops (including a supermarket), bars and restaurants. Prague 40 km. Karlovy Vary 10 km. Koniprusy caves.

Open: 24 April - 15 September.

Directions: From the west, take no. 6/E48 express road towards Prague. Site is close to this road, about 3 km. after the Revnicov exit and is clearly signed from this point. Coming from the east, ignore other camping signs and continue until Bucek is signed (to the north). GPS: 50.1728, 13.8348

Charges guide

Per unit incl. 2 persons and electricity	CZK 450 - 590
extra person	CZK 75 - 95
child (under 12 yrs)	CZK 50 - 60
dog	CZK 50 - 60

Reductions in low season.
No credit cards.

Autocamping Liptovsky Trnovec

SK-03222 Liptovsky Trnovec (Zilina)
t: 044 559 8458 e: atc.trnovec@atctrnovec.sk
alanrogers.com/SK4915 www.atctrnovec.sk

Accommodation: ☑Pitch ☑Mobile home/chalet ☐ Hotel/B&B ☐ Apartment

This is a good Slovakian site beside the Liptovská Mara reservoir, also close to the Tatra Mountains which are popular for climbing, hiking and mountain biking. The lake can be used for sailing, surfing, boating and pedaloes and some of this equipment may be rented on the site. Bicycles are also available for hire. There are 250 pitches, all used for touring units and with 14A electricity. With tarmac access roads, the level pitches are on a circular, grassy field and as pitching is rather haphazard, the site can become crowded in high season. Mature trees provide some shade, but in general this is an open site. There are several bars with snack and takeaway services on site with a restaurant nearby (300 m). The site is close to the historic cities of Liptovsky Mikulás (6 km), Vlkolinec (on the UNESCO World Heritage list) and Pribylina.

You might like to know

This site is situated on the banks of the Liptovská Mara dam, the largest in Slovakia. The reservoir is popular for lovers of water and outdoor sports. Liptovská Mara offers ideal conditions for yachting and windsurfing with the possibility of fishing, sightseeing trips and mountain bike routes.

- ☑ Mountain biking
- ☑ Sailing
- ☑ Windsurfing
- ☑ Golf
- ☑ Rafting
- ☑ Rock climbing
- ☑ Hiking
- ☑ Canoeing
- ☑ Kayaking
- ☑ Fishing

Facilities: Two good modern toilet blocks have British style toilets, washbasins in cabins and showers. Facilities for disabled visitors. Washing machines. Campers' kitchen. Bar with covered terrace and takeaway service. Basic playground. Minigolf. Fishing. Bicycle hire. Canoe hire and boat rental. Games room with arcade machines. Beach. Off site: New Tatralandia Aqua Park nearby. Walking in the Lower Tatra Mountains, or real climbing in the Higher Tatra Mountains.

Open: 1 May - 15 October.

Directions: From E50 road take exit for Liptovsky Mikulás and turn left towards Liptovsky Trnovec on 584 road. Continue alongside the lake to site on the left.
GPS: 49.111133, 19.54595

Charges guide

Per person	SKK 70 - 110
child (4-15 yrs)	SKK 25 - 60
pitch incl. car	SKK 105 - 220

Fårup Sø Camping

Fårupvej 58, DK-7300 Jelling (Vejle)
t: 75 87 13 44 e: faarup-soe@dk-camp.dk
alanrogers.com/DK2048 www.dk-camp.dk/faarup-soe

Accommodation: ☑Pitch ☑Mobile home/chalet ☐ Hotel/B&B ☐ Apartment

This site was originally set up on the woodlands of Jelling Skov where local farmers each had their own plot. Owned since January 2004 by the Dutch/Danish Albring family, this is a rural location on the Fårup Lake. Many of the trees have now been removed to give the site a welcoming, open feel. Fårup Sø Camping has 250 grassy pitches, mostly on terraces (from top to bottom the height difference is 53 m). The 35 newest terraced pitches provide beautiful views of the countryside and the Fårup lake. There are 200 pitches for touring units, most with 10A electricity, and some tent pitches without electricity. Next to the top toilet block is a barbecue area with a terrace and good views. A neighbour rents out water bikes and takes high season excursions onto the lake with a real Viking Ship which campers can join. During the last weekend of May, the site celebrates the Jelling Musical Festival when it is advisable to book in advance. This family site is ideal for those who want to enjoy a relaxed holiday on the lakeside beaches or go walking or cycling through the surrounding countryside.

You might like to know
There is an excellent animal park 8 km. from this site.

- ☑ Riding
- ☑ Pony trekking
- ☑ Cycling (road)
- ☑ Sports field
- ☑ Outdoor pool
- ☑ Golf
- ☑ Canoeing
- ☑ Pedaloes
- ☑ Fishing
- ☑ Boat launching

Facilities: One modern and one older toilet block have British style toilets, open style washbasins and controllable hot showers. Family shower rooms. Baby room. Facilities for disabled visitors. Laundry. Campers' kitchen. Motorcaravan services. Shop (bread to order). Outdoor heated swimming pool (15x5 m). Whirlpool. New playgrounds. Minigolf. Games room. Pony riding. Lake with fishing, watersports and Viking ship. Activities for children (high season). Internet. Off site: Golf and riding 2 km. Lion Park 8 km. Boat launching 10 km. Legoland 20 km.

Open: 1 April - 30 September.

Directions: From Vejle take the 28 road towards Billund. In Skibet turn right towards Fårup Sø, Jennum and Jelling and follow the signs to Fårup Sø. GPS: 55.73614, 9.41777

Charges guide

Per person	DKK 61
child (3-11 yrs)	DKK 35
pitch	DKK 15 - 35
electricity	DKK 28

Jesperhus Feriecenter & Camping

Legindvej 30, DK-7900 Nykobing Mors (Viborg)
t: **96 70 14 00** e: **jesperhus@jesperhus.dk**
alanrogers.com/DK2140 www.jesperhus.dk

Accommodation: ☑Pitch ☑Mobile home/chalet ☐ Hotel/B&B ☐ Apartment

Jesperhus is an extensive, well organised and busy site with many leisure activities, adjacent to Blomsterpark (flower park). It is a 'TopCamp' site with 662 numbered pitches, mostly in rows with some terracing, divided by shrubs and trees and with shade in parts. Many pitches are taken by seasonal, tour operator or rental units, so advance booking is advised for peak periods. Electricity (6A) is available on all pitches and water points are in all areas. With all the activities at this site an entire holiday could be spent here regardless of the weather, although Jesperhus is also an excellent centre for touring. The indoor and outdoor pool complex (daily charge) has three pools, diving boards, water slides with the 'Black Hole', spa pools, saunas and a solarium. Although it may appear to be just part of Jutland, Mors is an island in its own right surrounded by the lovely Limfjord. It is joined to the mainland by a fine 2,000 m. bridge at the end of which are signs to Blomsterpark (Northern Europe's largest flower park) and the campsite – both under the same ownership.

You might like to know
The indoor facilities provide a wide range of sport activities including squash and a climbing wall.

- ☑ Riding
- ☑ Tennis
- ☑ Cycling *(road)*
- ☑ Mountain biking
- ☑ Outdoor pool
- ☑ Golf
- ☑ Go-karting
- ☑ 10-pin bowling
- ☑ Fishing
- ☑ Beach volleyball

Facilities: Four good sanitary units are cleaned three times daily. Facilities include washbasins in cubicles or with divider/curtain, family and whirlpool bathrooms (on payment), suites for babies and disabled people. Free sauna. Superb kitchens and a fully equipped laundry. Supermarket (1/4-1/11). Restaurant. Bar. Café, takeaway. Pool complex with spa facilities. Bowling. Minigolf. Tennis. Go-karts and other outdoor sports. Children's 'play-world'. Playgrounds. Pets corner. Golf. Fishing pond. Practice golf (3 holes). Off site: Riding 2 km. Bicycle hire 6 km. Beach 2 km.

Open: All year.

Directions: From south or north, take road no. 26 to Salling Sund bridge, site is signed Jesperhus, just north of the bridge. GPS: 56.75082, 8.81580

Charges guide

Per person	DKK 75
child (1-11 yrs)	DKK 55
pitch	free - DKK 50
electricity	DKK 40

DENMARK – Fjerritslev

Klim Strand Camping

Havvejen 167, Klim Strand, DK-9690 Fjerritslev (Nordjylland)
t: 98 22 53 40   e: ksc@klim-strand.dk
alanrogers.com/DK2170   www.klim-strand.dk

Accommodation: ☑Pitch ☑Mobile home/chalet ☐Hotel/B&B ☐Apartment

A large family holiday site right beside the sea, Klim Strand is a paradise for children. It is a privately owned 'TopCamp' site with a full complement of quality facilities, including its own fire engine and trained staff. The site has 460 numbered touring pitches, all with electricity (10A), laid out in rows, many divided by trees and hedges and shade in parts. Some 220 of these are fully serviced with electricity, water, drainage and TV hook-up. On site activities include an outdoor water slide complex, an indoor pool, tennis courts and pony riding (all free). A 'Wellness' spa centre is a recent addition. For children there are numerous play areas, an adventure playground with aerial cable ride and a roller skating area. There is a kayak school and a large bouncy castle for toddlers. Live music and dancing are organised twice a week in high season. Suggested excursions include trips to offshore islands, visits to local potteries, a brewery museum and bird watching on the Bygholm Vejle. Member of Leading Campings Group.

You might like to know
The Oceanarium of the North Sea is the largest aquarium in the north of Europe.

- ☑ Riding
- ☑ Tennis
- ☑ Cycling *(road)*
- ☑ Outdoor pool
- ☑ Golf
- ☑ Kayaking
- ☑ Fitness/gym
- ☑ Fishing

Facilities: Two good, large, heated toilet blocks are central, with spacious showers and some washbasins in cubicles. Separate children's room. Baby rooms. Bathrooms for families (some charged) and disabled visitors. Two smaller units are by reception and beach. Laundry. Well equipped kitchens and barbecue areas. TV lounges. Motorcaravan services. Pizzeria. Supermarket, restaurant and bar (all season). Pool complex. Sauna, solariums, whirlpool bath, hairdressing rooms, fitness room. Wellness centre. Internet cafe. TV rental. Play areas. Crèche. Bicycle hire. Cabins to rent. Off site: Golf 10 km. Boat launching 25 km.

Open: 26 March - 24 October.

Directions: Turn off the Thisted - Fjerritslev no. 11 road to Klim from where site is signed. GPS: 57.133333, 9.166667

Charges guide

Per unit incl. 2 persons and electricity	DKK 305 - 355
extra person	DKK 75
child (1-11 yrs)	DKK 55
dog	DKK 25

DENMARK – Grenå

Fornæs Camping

Stensmarkvej 36, DK-8500 Grenå (Århus)
t: 86 33 23 30   e: fornaes@1031.inord.dk
alanrogers.com/DK2070

Accommodation: ☑Pitch ☑Mobile home/chalet ☐Hotel/B&B ☐Apartment

In the grounds of a former farm, Fornæs Camping is about 5 km. from Grenå. From reception a wide, gravel access road descends through a large grassy field to the sea. Pitches to the left are mostly level, to the right slightly sloping with some terracing and views of the Kattegat. The rows of pitches are divided into separate areas by colourful bushes and each row is marked by a concrete tub containing a young tree and colourful flowers. Fornæs has 320 pitches of which 240 are for tourers, the others being used for seasonal visitors. All touring pitches have 10A electricity. At the foot of the site is a pebble beach with a large grass area behind it for play and sunbathing. There is also an attractive outdoor pool with two slides, a paddling pool, sauna, solarium and whirlpool near the entrance. Here also, a comprehensive room serves as a restaurant, takeaway and bar, and in a former barn there is a new games room. Fornæs provides a good base from which to explore this part of Denmark or for taking the ferry to Hjelm island or to Sweden.

You might like to know
There are a number of attractive, fully equipped wooden chalets on this site, all available for rent.

☑ Riding
☑ Outdoor pool
☑ Sailing
☑ Golf
☑ Fishing
☑ Minigolf
☑ Sauna
☑ Adventure playground

Facilities: Two toilet blocks have British style toilets, washbasins in cabins and controllable hot showers (on payment). Child-size toilets. Family shower rooms. Baby room. Facilities for disabled people. Fully equipped laundry. Campers' kitchen. Motorcaravan service point. Shop. Café/grill with bar and takeaway (evenings). Swimming pool (80 m²) with paddling pool. Sauna and solarium. Play area and adventure playground. Games room with satellite TV. Minigolf. Fishing. Watersports. Off site: Golf and riding 5 km.

Open: 15 March - 20 September.

Directions: From Århus follow the 15 road towards Grenå and then the 16 road towards town centre. Turn north and follow signs for Fornæs and the site. GPS: 56.45602, 10.94107

Charges guide

Per person	DKK 67 - 75
child (1-12 yrs)	DKK 38 - 42
electricity (10A)	DKK 28

Credit cards 5% surcharge.

Odda Camping

Borsto, N-5750 Odda (Hordaland)
t: 41 32 16 10   e: post@oppleve.no
alanrogers.com/NO2320   www.oppleve.no

Accommodation: ☑Pitch ☑Mobile home/chalet ☐Hotel/B&B ☐Apartment

Bordered by the Folgefonna glacier to the west and the Hardangervidda plateau to the east and south, Odda is an industrial town with electro-chemical enterprises based on zinc mining and hydro-electric power. This site has been attractively developed on the town's southern outskirts. It is spread over 2.5 acres of flat, mature woodland, which is divided into small clearings by massive boulders. Access is by well tended tarmac roads which wind their way among the trees and boulders. There are 55 touring pitches including 36 with electricity. The site fills up in the evenings and can be crowded with facilities stretched from the end of June to early August. The site is just over a kilometre from the centre on the shores of the Sandvin lake (good salmon and trout fishing) and on the minor road leading up the Buar Valley to the Buar glacier, Vidfoss Falls and Folgefonna ice cap. It is possible to walk to the ice face but in the later stages this is quite hard going!

You might like to know
The campsite is open all year offering varied opportunities for new experiences and increased knowledge of nature and outdoor life – these include winter orienteering and tours to waterfalls, glaciers etc.

- ☑ Riding
- ☑ Tennis
- ☑ Mountain biking
- ☑ Archery
- ☑ Paintball
- ☑ Rafting
- ☑ Rock climbing
- ☑ Hiking
- ☑ Skiing *(downhill)*
- ☑ Snowboarding

- ☑ Canoeing
- ☑ Water rugby
- ☑ Glacier walks
- ☑ Fishing
- ☑ Lake swimming

Facilities: A single timber building at the entrance houses the reception office and the simple, but clean sanitary facilities which provide, for each sex, 2 WCs, one hot shower (on payment) and 3 open washbasins. A new building provides additional unisex toilets, showers and laundry facilities. Small kitchen with dishwashing facilities. Mini shop. Off site: Town facilities close.

Open: All year.

Directions: Site is on the southern outskirts of Odda, signed off road to Buar, with a well marked access. GPS: 60.05320, 6.54380

Charges guide

Per person	NOK 10
tent and car	NOK 110
caravan or motorcaravan	NOK 130
electricity	NOK 40

No credit cards.

NORWAY – Lærdal

Lærdal Ferie & Fritidspark

Grandavegens, N-6886 Lærdal (Sogn og Fjordane)
t: **57 66 66 95**   e: **info@laerdalferiepark.com**
alanrogers.com/NO2375   **www.laerdalferiepark.com**

Accommodation: ☑Pitch ☐ Mobile home/chalet ☑Hotel/B&B ☑Apartment

This site is beside the famous Sognefjord, the longest fjord in the world. It is ideally situated if you want to explore the glaciers, fjords and waterfalls of the region. The 100 pitches are level with well trimmed grass and connected by tarmac roads and are suitable for tents, caravans and motorcaravans. There are 80 electrical hook-ups. The fully licensed restaurant serves traditional meals as well as snacks and pizzas. The pretty little village of Lærdal, only 400 m. away, is well worth a visit. A walk among the old, small wooden houses is a pleasant and interesting experience. You can hire boats on the site for short trips on the fjord. Guided hiking, cycling and fishing trips are also available. The site also provides cabins, flats and rooms to rent, plus a brand new motel, all very modern and extremely tastefully designed.

You might like to know

The Norwegian Wild Salmon Centre is 400 m.

- ☑ Riding
- ☑ Tennis
- ☑ Cycling (road)
- ☑ Mountain biking
- ☑ Golf
- ☑ Hiking
- ☑ Canoeing
- ☑ Fishing
- ☑ Beach volleyball

Facilities: Two modern and well decorated sanitary blocks with washbasins (some in cubicles), showers on payment, and toilets. Facilities for disabled visitors. Children's room. Washing machine and dryer. Kitchen. Motorcaravan services. Small shop. Bar, restaurant and takeaway (20/5-5/9). TV room. Playground. Motorboats, rowing boats, canoes, bicycles and pedal cars for hire. Bicycle hire. Fishing. Internet (WiFi) at reception. Off site: Cruises on the Sognefjord 400 m. Riding 500 m. Golf 12 km. The Flåm railway 40 km.

Open: All year,
by telephone request 1 Nov - 14 March.

Directions: Site is on road 5 (from the Oslo - Bergen road, E 16) 400 m. north of Lærdal village centre. GPS: 61.09977, 7.46962

Charges guide

Per unit incl. 2 persons and electricity	NOK 210
extra person	NOK 50
child (4-15 yrs)	NOK 25

NORWAY – Sogndal

Kjørnes Camping

N-6856 Sogndal (Sogn og Fjordane)
t: 57 67 45 80 e: camping@kjornes.no
alanrogers.com/NO2390 www.kjornes.no

Accommodation: ☑Pitch ☑Mobile home/chalet ☐ Hotel/B&B ☑Apartment

Kjørnes Camping is idyllically situated on the Sognefjord, 3 km. from the centre of Sogndal. It occupies a long open meadow which is terraced down to the waterside. The site has 100 pitches for camping units (all with electricity), 9 cabins and 2 apartments for rent. Located at the very centre of the 'fjord kingdom' by the main no. 5 road, this site is the ideal base from which to explore the Sognefjord. You are within a short drive (maximum one hour) from all the major attractions including the Jostedal glacier, the Nærøyfjord, the Flåm Railway, the Urnes Stave Church and Sognefjellet. This site is ideal for those who enjoy peace and quiet, lovely scenery or a spot of fishing. Access is via a narrow lane with passing places, which drops down towards the fjord three kilometres from Sogndal.

You might like to know

The Sogn Folkemuseum is an activity museum for all ages, that exhibits old homes, buildings and farm animals and shows how the local farmers worked the land in the 1800s.

- ☑ **Cycling** *(road)*
- ☑ **Mountain biking**
- ☑ **Rafting**
- ☑ **Rock climbing**
- ☑ **Hiking**
- ☑ **Aerial walkways**
- ☑ **Fishing**
- ☑ **Glacier walks**
- ☑ **Swimming**
- ☑ **Local sports hall**

Facilities: A new, high quality sanitary building was added in 2008. Baby room. Facilities for disabled visitors. A new building provides a kitchen with cooking facilities, dishwasher, a dining area overlooking the fjord, and laundry facilities. Small shop (20/6-20/8). Satellite TV, WiFi and internet. Off site: Hiking, glacier walks, climbing, rafting, walking around Sognefjord. Details from reception. Bicycle hire 3 km.

Open: 1 May - 1 October.

Directions: Site is off the Rv 5, 3 km. east of Sogndal, 8 km. west of Kaupanger. GPS: 61.21123, 7.12105

Charges guide

Per unit incl. 2 persons and electricity	NOK 260
extra person	NOK 30
child (4-16 yrs)	NOK 10

Trollveggen Camping

Horgheimseidet, N-6300 Åndalsnes (Møre og Romsdal)
t: 71 22 37 00   e: post@trollveggen.no
alanrogers.com/NO2452   www.trollveggen.no

Accommodation: ☑Pitch ☑Mobile home/chalet ☐ Hotel/B&B ☐ Apartment

The location of this site provides a unique experience – it is set at the foot of the famous vertical cliff of Trollveggen (the Troll Wall), which is Europe's highest vertical mountain face. The site is pleasantly laid out in terraces with level grass pitches. The facility block, the four cabins and the reception are all very attractively built with grass roofs. Beside the river is an attractive barbecue area where barbecue parties are sometimes arranged. This site is a must for people who love nature. The site is surrounded by the Troll Peaks and the Romsdalshorn Mountains with the rapid river of Rauma flowing by. Here in the beautiful valley of Romsdalen you have the ideal starting point for trips to many outstanding attractions such as 'The Troll Road' to Geiranger or to the Mandalsfossen waterfalls. In the mountains there are nature trails of various lengths and difficulties. The campsite owners are happy to help you with information. The town of Åndalsnes is 10 km. away and has a long tourism tradition as a place to visit. It is situated in the inner part of the beautiful Romsdal fjord and has a range of shops and restaurants.

You might like to know
A popular attraction is the Atlanterhavsveien, a spectular scenic road that winds its way along the coast between rocky outcrops and islands. Voted Norwegian construction of the century.

- ☑ Mountain biking
- ☑ Outdoor pool
- ☑ Golf
- ☑ Rock climbing
- ☑ Hiking
- ☑ Fishing
- ☑ Glacier walking
- ☑ Paragliding
- ☑ Base jumping

Facilities: One heated toilet block provides washbasins, some in cubicles, and showers on payment. Family room with baby bath and changing mat, plus facilities for disabled visitors. Communal kitchen with cooking rings, small ovens, fridge and sinks (free hot water). Laundry facilities. Motorcaravan service point. Barbecue area (covered). Playground. Duck pond. Off site: Climbing, glacier walking and hiking. Fjord fishing. The Troll Road. Mardalsfossen (waterfall). Geiranger and Åndalsnes.

Open: 10 May - 20 September.

Directions: Site is located on the E136 road, 10 km. south of Åndalsnes. It is signed. GPS: 62.49444, 7.758333

Charges guide

Per unit incl. 2 persons and electricity	NOK 190 - 210
extra person (over 4 yrs)	NOK 10

NORWAY – Byglandsfjord

Neset Camping

N-4741 Byglandsfjord (Aust-Agder)
t: 37 93 42 55 e: post@neset.no
alanrogers.com/NO2610 www.neset.no

Accommodation: ☑Pitch ☑Mobile home/chalet ☐ Hotel/B&B ☐ Apartment

On a semi-promontory on the shores of the 40 km. long Byglandsfjord, Neset is a good centre for activities or as a stop en route north from the ferry port of Kristiansand (from England or Denmark). Neset is situated on well kept grassy meadows by the lake shore with the water on three sides and the road on the fourth, and provides 200 unmarked pitches with electricity and cable TV available. The main building houses reception, a small shop and a restaurant with fine views over the water. This is a well run, friendly site where one could spend an active few days. Byglandsfjord offers good fishing (mainly trout) and the area has marked trails for cycling, riding or walking in an area famous for its minerals.

You might like to know
The Setesdal valley is home to a number of museums devoted to silver craft and other minerals as well as art and handicraft.

- ☑ Riding
- ☑ Cycling (road)
- ☑ Mountain biking
- ☑ Sailing
- ☑ Rafting
- ☑ Rock climbing
- ☑ Hiking
- ☑ Canoeing
- ☑ Fishing
- ☑ Skiing
  (cross-country)

Facilities: Three modern sanitary blocks which can be heated, all with comfortable hot showers (some on payment), washing up facilities (metered hot water) and a kitchen. Restaurant and takeaway (15/6-15/8). Shop (1/5-1/10). Campers' kitchen. Playground. Lake swimming, boating and fishing. Excellent new barbecue area and hot tub. Bicycle, canoe and pedalo hire. Climbing, rafting and canoeing courses arranged (including trips to see beavers and elk). Cross-country skiing possible in winter. Off site: Rock climbing wall. Marked forest trails.

Open: All year.

Directions: Site is on route 9, 2.5 km. north of the town of Byglandsfjord on the eastern shores of the lake. GPS: 58.68848, 7.80132

Charges guide

Per person	NOK 10
pitch	NOK 160
child (5-12 yrs)	NOK 5
electricity	NOK 30

Röstånga Camping & Bad

Blinkarpsvägen 3, S-260 24 Röstånga (Skåne Län)
t: 043 591 064   e: nystrand@msn.com
alanrogers.com/SW2630   www.rostangacamping.se

Accommodation: ☑Pitch ☑Mobile home/chalet ☐ Hotel/B&B ☐ Apartment

Beside the Söderåsen National Park, this scenic campsite has its own fishing lake and many activities for the whole family. There are now 136 large, level, grassy pitches with electricity (10A) and a quiet area for tents with a view over the fishing lake. The tent area has its own service building and several barbecue places. A large holiday home and 14 pleasant cabins are available to rent all year round. A pool complex adjacent to the site provides a 50 metre swimming pool, three children's pools and a water slide, all heated during peak season. Activities are arranged on the site in high season, including a children's club with exciting activities such as treasure hunts and gold panning, and for adults, aquarobics, Nordic walking and tennis. The Söderåsen National Park offers hiking and bicycle trails. The friendly staff will be happy to help you to plan interesting excursions in the area.

Special offers
There is a guided tour in the National park for all campers – free of charge in high season.

You might like to know
An activity leader arranges a wide selection of activities and events – free of charge for all campers.

☑ Riding
☑ Pony trekking
☑ Tennis
☑ Cycling *(road)*
☑ Mountain biking
☑ Outdoor pool
☑ Golf
☑ Hiking
☑ Canoeing
☑ Fishing

Facilities: Four good, heated sanitary blocks with free hot water and facilities for babies and disabled visitors. Laundry with washing machines and dryers. Kitchen with cooking rings, oven and microwave. Motorcaravan service point. Small shop at reception. Bar, restaurant and takeaway. Minigolf. Tennis. Fitness trail. Fishing. Canoe hire. Children's club. WiFi. Off site: Swimming pool complex adjacent to site (free for campers as is a visit to the Zoo). Many golf courses nearby. Motor racing track at Ring Knutstorp 8 km.

Open: 9 April - 18 October.

Directions: From Malmö: drive towards Lund and follow road no. 108 to Röstånga. From Stockholm: turn off at Østra Ljungby and take road no. 13 to Röstånga. In Röstånga drive through the village on road no. 108 and follow the signs. GPS: 55.996583, 13.28005

Charges guide

Per unit incl. 2 persons and electricity	SEK 200 - 295

SWEDEN – Uddevalla

Hafsten Swecamp Resort

Hafsten 120, S-451 96 Uddevalla (Västra Götalands Län)
t: 052 264 4117 e: info@hafsten.se
alanrogers.com/SW2725 www.hafsten.se

Accommodation: ☑Pitch ☑Mobile home/chalet ☐Hotel/B&B ☐Apartment

This privately owned site on the west coast is situated on a peninsula overlooking the magnificent coastline of Bohuslän. Open all year, it is a lovely terraced site with a beautiful, shallow and child-friendly sandy beach and many nature trails in the vicinity. There are 180 touring pitches, all with electricity (10A), 70 of them with water and drainage. In all, there are 330 pitches including a tent area and 60 cottages of a high standard. There are plenty of activities available including, canoeing, fishing, horse riding, minigolf, tennis, clay pigeon shooting, water slide and a paddling pool (charged), boat and motor boat hire. Troubadour evenings are arranged during the summer. Almost any activity can be arranged on the site or elsewhere by the friendly owners if they are given advance notice. Amenities include two clean and well maintained service buildings, a pub, a fully licensed restaurant with wine from their own French vineyard, and a well stocked shop (all open all year) and a takeaway (1/6-31/8).

You might like to know
The site is located between Stromstad and Gothenburg and is open all year.

☑ Riding
☑ Tennis
☑ Cycling (road)
☑ Mountain biking
☑ Crafts
☑ Sailing
☑ Golf
☑ Hiking
☑ Canoeing
☑ Fishing

Facilities: Two heated sanitary buildings provide the usual facilities. Showers are on payment. Kitchen with good cooking facilities and dishwashing sinks. Dining room. Laundry facilities. Units for disabled visitors. Motorcaravan services. Shop. Restaurant, takeaway and pub. Troubadour evenings. TV room. Relaxation centre with sauna and jacuzzi (charged). Water slide (charged). Internet access (WiFi). Riding. Minigolf. Tennis. Playground. Off site: Nordens Ark (animal park) 40 km. Havets hus (marine museum) 30 km. Golf 13 km. Shopping centre 13 km.

Open: All year.

Directions: From the E6, north Uddevalla, at Torpmotet exit take the 161 road towards Lysekil. At the Rotviksbro roundabout take the 161 road towards Orust. The exit to the site is located further on road 2 km. on the left. Follow the signs for 4 km. It is a narrow, one way road for motorcaravans and caravans.
GPS: 58.314683, 11.723333

Charges guide

Per pitch incl. electricity	SEK 210 - 330

Bredäng Camping Stockholm

Stora Sällskapets väg, S-127 31 Skärholmen (Stockholms Län)
t: **089 770 71** e: **bredangcamping@telia.com**
alanrogers.com/SW2842 www.bredangcamping.se

Accommodation: ☑Pitch ☑Mobile home/chalet ☐Hotel/B&B ☐Apartment

Bredäng is a busy city site, with easy access to Stockholm city centre. Large and fairly level, with very little shade, there are 380 pitches, including 115 with hardstanding and 204 with electricity (10A), and a separate area for tents. Reception is open from 08.00-23.00 in the main season (12/6-20/8), reduced hours in low season, and English is spoken. A Stockholm card is available, or a three-day public transport card at the Tube station. Stockholm has many events and activities, you can take a circular tour on a free sightseeing bus, various boat and bus tours, or view the city from the Kaknäs Tower (155 m). The nearest Tube station is five minutes' walk, trains run about every ten minutes between 05.00 and 02.00, and the journey takes about twenty minutes. The local shopping centre is five minutes away and a two minute walk through the woods brings you to a very attractive lake and beach.

You might like to know
Easy access to Stockholm but very close to Lake Malaren and just 350 m. from an open-air swimming area.

☑ Riding
☑ Tennis
☑ Cycling *(road)*
☑ Crafts
☑ Sailing
☑ Golf
☑ Hiking
☑ Canoeing
☑ Fishing

Facilities: Four heated sanitary units of a high standard provide British style WCs, controllable hot showers, with some washbasins in cubicles. One has a baby room, a unit for disabled people and a first aid room. Cooking and dishwashing facilities are in three units around the site. Laundry facilities. Motorcaravan services and car wash. Well stocked shop, bar, takeaway and fully licensed restaurant (all 1/5-31/8). Sauna. Playground. Bicycle hire. Off site: Fishing 500 m.

Open: April - October.

Directions: Site is about 10 km. southwest of city centre. Turn off E4/E20 at Bredängs signpost and follow clearly marked site signs. GPS: 59.29560, 17.92315

Charges guide

Per person	SEK 95 - 120
pitch	SEK 190 - 240
electricity	SEK 40

Discounts for pensioners in low season.

FINLAND – Ruovesi

Camping Haapasaaren Lomakylä

Haapasaarentie 5, FIN-34600 Ruovesi (Häme)
t: 044 080 0290 e: **lomakyla@haapasaari.fi**
alanrogers.com/FI2840 www.ruovedenhaapasaarenmatkailu.fi

Accommodation: ☑Pitch ☑Mobile home/chalet ☐ Hotel/B&B ☐ Apartment

Haapasaaren is located on Lake Näsijärvi, around 70 km. north of Tampere in south western Finland. This is a well equipped site with a café and restaurant, a traditional Finnish outside dancing area and, of course, plenty of saunas! Rowing boats, canoes, cycles and, during the winter months, sleds are all available for rent. Fishing is very popular here. Pitches are grassy and of a good size. There is also a good range of accommodation to rent, including holiday cottages with saunas. The cosy restaurant, Jätkäinkämppä, has an attractive terrace and fine views across the lake. Alternatively, the site's café offers a range of snacks as well as internet access. Haapasaaren's friendly owners organize a series of guided tours throughout the year. These include hiking and nature treks, berry and mushroom picking, and, during the winter, ice fishing and cross-country skiing. Helvetinjärvi National Park is one of the most dramatic areas of western Finland, and is made up of deep gorges and dense forests. There is a rich population of birds and occasionally even brown bears and lynx can be seen here.

You might like to know
Some great organised trips are on offer – try the berry and mushroom-picking trips, cross-country skiing or maybe even ice fishing and burbot catching!

- ☑ Mountain biking
- ☑ Sports field
- ☑ Skiing *(downhill)*
- ☑ Skiing *(cross-country)*
- ☑ Canoeing
- ☑ Fishing
- ☑ Rowing boats
- ☑ Nordic walking
- ☑ Sledging
- ☑ Sauna

Facilities: Café. Restaurant. Direct lake access. Saunas. Fishing. Minigolf. Boat and canoe hire. Bicycle hire. Guided tours. Play area. Tourist information. Chalets for rent. Off site: Walking and cycle routes. Boat trips. Helvetinjärvi National Park.

Open: All year.

Directions: From Helsinki, head north on the E12 motorway to Tampere and then northeast on N63-9 to Orivesi. Then, continue north on road 66 to Ruovesi and follow signs to the site. GPS: 61.99413, 24.069843

Charges guide

Per unit incl. 2 persons and electricity	€ 25,00
extra person	€ 4,00
child (under 15 yrs)	€ 2,00

FINLAND – Oulu

Nallikari Camping

PL55, FIN-90015 Oulu (Oulu)
t: 085 586 1350   e: nallikari.camping@ouka.fi
alanrogers.com/FI2970   www.nallikari.fi/FI/etusivu.html

Accommodation: ☑Pitch ☑Mobile home/chalet ☐ Hotel/B&B ☐ Apartment

This is probably one of the best sites in Scandinavia, set in a recreational wooded area alongside a sandy beach on the banks of the Baltic Sea, with the added bonus of the adjacent Eden Spa complex. Nallikari provides 200 pitches with electricity (some also have water supply and drainage), plus an additional 79 cottages to rent, 28 of which are suitable for winter occupation. Oulu is a modern town about 100 miles south of the Arctic Circle that enjoys long, sunny and dry summer days. The Baltic however is frozen for many weeks in the winter and then the sun barely rises for two months. In early June the days are very long with the sun setting at about 11.30pm and rising at 1.30 am! Nallikari, to the west of Oulu, is 3 km. along purpose built cycle paths and the town has much to offer. Nordic walking, with or without roller blades, seems to be a recreational pastime for Finns of all ages! You might even be tempted to buy a pair of these long brightly coloured walking sticks yourself!

You might like to know

Great spa facilities here. Or maybe you could try the Finnish custom of organising a meeting using the sauna facilities!

☑ **Tennis**
☑ **Cycling** (road)
☑ **Golf**
☑ **Hiking**
☑ **Skiing** (downhill)
☑ **Aerial walkways**
☑ **Fishing**
☑ **Squash**
☑ **Beach volleyball**

Facilities: The modern shower/WC blocks also provide male and female saunas, kitchen and launderette facilities. Facilities for disabled visitors. Motorcaravan service point. Playground. Reception with café/restaurant, souvenir and grocery shop. TV room. WiFi. Bicycle hire. Off site: The adjacent Eden centre provides excellent modern spa facilities where you can enjoy a day under the glass-roofed pool with its jacuzzis, saunas, Turkish baths and an Irish bath. Fishing 5 km. Golf 15 km.

Open: All year.

Directions: Leave route 4/E75 at junction with route 20 and head west down Kiertotie. Site well signed, Nallikari Eden, but continue on, just after traffic lights, cross a bridge and take the second on the right. Just before the Eden Complex turn right towards Lerike and reception.
GPS: 65.02973, 25.41793

Charges guide

Per unit incl. 2 persons	€ 9,00 - € 18,00
extra person	€ 4,00
child (under 15 yrs)	€ 1,00
electricity	€ 4,00 - € 6,00

Been to any good campsites lately?
We have

You'll find them here...

The UK's market leading independent guides to the best campsites

...and, new for 2011, here...

101 great campsites, ideal for your specific hobby, pastime or passion

Want independent campsite reviews at your fingertips?

You'll find them here...

Over 3,000 in-depth campsite reviews at **www.alanrogers.com**

...and even here...

An exciting free app from iTunes and the Apple app store*

*available January 2011

Want to book your holiday on one of Europe's top campsites?

We can do it for you. No problem.

The best campsites in the most popular regions - we'll take care of everything

alan rogers ⊘ travel

Discover the best campsites in Europe
with Alan Rogers

alanrogers.com
01580 214000

index

index

Associació de Càmpings
DE SANT PERE PESCADOR

Paradise under a blue sky

Discover Sant Pere Pescador's campsites

Located on the Costa Brava, Sant Pere Pescador sits between the sea and the mountains, part of the Empordà Natural Park. It's the only stretch on the Costa Brava with over 6 km of pristine sandy dunes, leading to the warm, shimmering waters of the Mediterranean. You'll find a choice of great family campsites, offering all kinds of activities, watersports, hiking, riding and cycling, as well as great swimming pools, restaurants and services.

Environmental conservation

The ACSPP campsites aim to protect the remarkable environment that surrounds them - many have achieved the EMAS certificate and ISO 1400.

www.acspp.org

Càmping Aquarius
Platja, s/n.
17470 Sant Pere Pescador. Girona
t: **(0034) 972 520 003**
f: **(0034) 972 550 216**
www.aquarius.es

Càmping La Ballena Alegre
17470 Sant Pere Pescador. Girona.
t: **(0034) 902 510 520**
f: **(0034) 902 510 521**
www.ballena-alegre.com

Càmping Las Dunas
17470 Sant Pere Pescador. Girona.
t: **(0034) 972 521 717**
f: **(0034) 972 550 046**
www.campinglasdunas.com

Càmping La Gaviota
Carretera de la Platja, s/n.
17470 Sant Pere Pescador. Girona.
t: **(0034) 972 520 569**
f: **(0034) 972 550 348**
www.lagaviota.com

Càmping Las Palmeras
Carretera de la Platja, s/n.
17470 Sant Pere Pescador. Girona.
t: **(0034) 972 520 506**
f: **(0034) 972 550 285**
www.campinglaspalmeras.com